LIVING
in the
SPIRIT

*drawing us
to God*

*sending us
to the world*

George O. Wood

with **Randy Hurst**

GPH GOSPEL PUBLISHING HOUSE
SPRINGFIELD, MISSOURI

03-7955

7th Printing 2013

CONTENTS

EORGE WOOD'S RESPECT FOR THE SPIRIT'S
LEADING WAS EXEMPLIFIED in the first General
Presbytery meeting he chaired as general superintendent. The devotional speaker that morning was an
evangelist in one of our Assemblies of God ethnic fellowships. At the end of his passionate message, the pres-
byters responded with vocal expressions of praise.

As Dr. Wood resumed the chair for a full morning
of church business, he paused and said, "I believe the
Spirit is doing something very special in our hearts. I
realize that when we get together we have a big docket to
go through and many agenda items. But when the
leaders of the Early Church got together, they spent time
praying. I want this General Presbytery meeting to
become a prayer meeting for awhile. If the Lord lays a
burden of intercession on your heart—for our country,
the Assemblies of God, our young people, our churches,
our pastors, our missionaries—and as the Spirit prompts
you, go to the microphones. Let's take some time and
open our hearts in corporate prayer."

For well over an hour, pastors and district leaders
stepped to the microphone. As I listened to the inspired
prayers interspersed with exhortations and guidance

from Dr. Wood, I couldn't help but feel it was an atmosphere in which the Assemblies of God founders would have felt at home.

As the one-hundred-year anniversary of the Assemblies of God approaches, this is an especially appropriate time for a fresh affirmation of Pentecostal theology and an invigorated pursuit of its application, both in the church and in our personal lives.

In a survey by the Evangelism Commission, pastors were asked what resources they felt were most needed to assist them in ministry. Of the nearly one thousand responses received, one of the most frequently mentioned items was material concerning the breadth of purpose of Spirit baptism and instruction on encouraging people to seek and receive the Spirit's fullness.

Dr. Wood's book is especially significant and timely in its theme and the instruction it provides. An appropriate sequel to his book *Core Values*, *Living in the Spirit* conveys the truths, values and commitment that compelled our Pentecostal forefathers and emphasizes our vital need for living in the Spirit in today's world.

The book's subtitle, "drawing us to God . . . sending us to the world," was taken from Dr. Wood's analysis in chapter 3. He reminds us that living in the Spirit affects personal spirituality—both in worship and in witness—as it brings us into greater intimacy with God and equips us to proclaim the message of Jesus in the world.

As you read this book, you will sense Dr. Wood's concern that Pentecostals today not be content with memories of powerful past encounters with the Spirit and fail to seek, as Dr. Wood expresses in chapters 2 and 3, being "overwhelmed by the Spirit" and demonstrating the "enduring evidence" of His fullness. He states our need succinctly in chapter 2: "God would have His Spirit call us out of a life of spiritual complacency to one of deep surrender."

While *Core Values* was based entirely on interviews, *Living in the Spirit* was assembled from a variety of sources, beginning with six transcribed sermons on the Holy Spirit that he preached while pastor of Newport-Mesa Christian Center in Costa Mesa, California. A prolific thinker and writer, Dr. Wood emailed observations and insights to me throughout this project—even in the final week before printing. Each addition was so meaningful that it found a place in the book, much to the reader's benefit. Supplemental content was gathered from articles and columns he has written over the years. The book was completed with a series of interviews. One interview was videotaped, and a portion of it can be seen on a special Web site, www.LivingintheSpirit.ag.org. The chapters vary in style due to the sources from which the teachings and insights were drawn.

Pastors' priorities and effectiveness become obvious to the pastors who follow them, which is why I asked Dr. James Bradford, his successor at Newport-Mesa Christian Center, to share his insights on Dr. Wood's leadership concerning the Spirit's ministry in a local church context.

Living in the Spirit offers inspiration and instruction concerning the vital role of the Holy Spirit's presence in life and ministry. Though the book is not intended to be an exhaustive treatment of Pentecostal doctrine, it offers a comprehensive compilation of perspectives from the leader of our Fellowship. As I interviewed Dr. Wood, his spontaneous responses clearly revealed the scope and depth of his knowledge of the Scriptures and the history of the Pentecostal movement. Dr. Wood's ability to express orthodox Pentecostal theology in creative and refreshing ways is unique. I believe his many insights in this book will incite readers both to study the Scriptures and increasingly to seek the Spirit's enablement.

—RANDY HURST

*Assemblies of God Commissioner of Evangelism &
Communications Director of AG World Missions*

I F YOU WANT TO LEARN WHAT A PASTOR IS REALLY LIKE, FOLLOW THAT PERSON AS THE *NEXT* PASTOR. In the summer of 1988 my wife, our nine-month-old daughter, and I moved to Southern California to follow Dr. George O. Wood as the next pastor of Newport-Mesa Christian Center. Under Dr. Wood's seventeen years of pastoral leadership, the church had grown from a few dozen people to more than two thousand adherents.

Dr. Wood had already distinguished himself across the country as a brilliant biblical expositor. His election to district office, however, created a vacancy at the church that launched one of the most life-stretching adventures of my life. In the process, I learned a lot about the spirituality of the man I followed.

My first glimpse into his sensitivity to the Holy Spirit came from the pastoral search process itself. A mutual friend had shared my name with Dr. Wood as a possible pastoral candidate. At the time, I was pastoring a much smaller university church on the edge of the Minneapolis campus of the University of Minnesota. Dr. Wood later told me that when he considered my name, he experienced a marked sense of the Holy Spirit speaking to his spirit that

I was the one to pastor the church—even though he had no idea who I was.

I turned down the invitation twice, but Dr. Wood remained unmoved in his conviction. I had fears and misgivings but he had heard from the Lord. That impressed me. I served at Newport-Mesa for twelve years.

A year or two after I became pastor, I attended a sectional business meeting Dr. Wood was helping to lead. I will never forget him giving a powerful prophetic word during the gathering. I can still remember some of what he said. It impressed me that he would carry forward into his broader leadership role a foundational connection to the Holy Spirit, obviously nurtured during his years as a pastor.

It was not unusual, in fact, to hear stories anecdotally from church members about Dr. Wood's responsiveness to the Spirit as he touched their life. Sometimes God prompted him to call or visit people at particularly critical moments, or gave him discernment into people and their intentions that only the Lord could give. Dr. Wood also seemed to have a gift of faith for what was needed next, along with a high regard for prophetic words that were given from time to time in the life of the congregation.

When I arrived at the church it was, unsurprisingly, strong and healthy. The congregation was much larger and more multigenerational and traditional in style than the university church I had left. The authentic work of the Holy Spirit, however, was very much present. I found the congregation to be comprised of people from a variety of Christian and non-Christian backgrounds.

They were drawn by Dr. Wood's teaching ministry but they had also grown in a hunger for God and a deep desire to worship and serve Him. It was a congregation that had joy and vitality.

It was not unusual to witness the vocal gifts of the Spirit in operation in the services, as well as other gifts of the Spirit working through people's lives. For years, Dr. Wood had intentionally carved out time in the three Sunday morning services for people to be prayed for personally at the altar. It was faith building to hear stories of people being healed and freed by Christ's power during those years.

The church was also very missions minded and focused. The purpose of Pentecost is, of course, world evangelization. To be Pentecostal is to be worldwide in vision and ministry, engaged at both a local and global level. That was certainly the case at Newport-Mesa under Dr. Wood's leadership. There were many volunteers in the church and the congregation supported a large number of missionaries.

It was also evident that the church had been exposed to very solid and balanced teaching concerning the person and ministry of the Holy Spirit. Whether it was Spirit baptism, the ministry of the spiritual gifts, or the work of the Spirit in the daily life of believers, Dr. Wood had taught clearly, systematically and effectively. The substance of some of that teaching is reflected in this book.

The material within these pages is, in fact, an authentic extension of what Dr. Wood believed and lived himself as a pastor. His humility and spiritual track record make credible all that he continues to teach on the person and work of the Holy Spirit in his present leadership role. May you, too, catch the spirit of his heart and find yourself even more hungry for God as you read this book and open your heart again to the Spirit's work.

—DR. JAMES BRADFORD
General Secretary of the Assemblies of God

[FOREWORD]

I RECENTLY BECAME A FATHER. GEORGE REESE WOOD WAS BORN ON SUNDAY, OCTOBER 26, 2008. Before his birth, we referred to him as G4, because he is the fourth *George Wood* in a row.

- G1 is George Roy Wood, born February 26, 1908
- G2 is George Oliver Wood, born September 1, 1941
- G3 is George Paul Wood, born May 8, 1969
- G4 is George Reese Wood, born October 26, 2008

As you can see, the four Georges have something in common: their first and last names. But their middle names are different, giving them some individuality. Unlike G1 through G3, however, G4 doesn't go by the name George. He goes by Reese. His first name is his heritage. It doesn't exhaust who he is, or how he is perceived by others.

I think about Pentecostalism in the same way. I am a third-generation Assemblies of God minister. G1 was a pioneering missionary and small-church pastor. G2 was a large-church pastor and is a denominational leader. I am the pastor of a small turnaround church. We share some things in common: doctrine, mission and experience. But we also do things very differently from one another.

Some of our differences are *methodological*: suits vs. Hawaiian shirts in the pulpit, organs vs. drums in the song service, and a variety of ways for persons to respond at the close of the service.

Some of our differences are *generational*. In G1's generation, the leadership model was command-and-control. Authority flowed from the top down. In my generation, anyone with a blog can challenge authority, so authority has to be earned and then shared.

But some of our differences are *substantial*. G1 was trained in a small Pentecostal Bible college and finished his theological education by correspondence. My dad attended an Assemblies of God liberal arts college and then a non-Pentecostal seminary because in his day the AG did not have a seminary. I did not attend an AG school because none had the major I needed. These educational experiences shaped our outlooks on life.

When my dad was elected general superintendent of the Assemblies of God in August 2007, he immediately invited a group of young AG ministers to come to Springfield, Missouri, for a daylong dialogue about pressing issues in our Movement. The highlight was a dinner at my parents' home, followed by several hours of discussion and prayer. Most of the questions dealt with Articles 7 and 8 of our Fellowship's Statement of Fundamental Truths concerning Spirit baptism and initial evidence.

Some people are easily offended when you ask hard questions about long-settled doctrines. My dad isn't. He welcomes questions. How can you "contend for the faith that was once for all entrusted to the saints" (Jude 3) if you don't bother to answer the questions people ask about it? And so, throughout that night's dialogue, my dad articulated, defended, and drew out the implications of our Movement's distinctive doctrines.

As I read *Living in the Spirit*, I hear a lot of what my dad said to the ministers that night echoing through its pages. You will find an able defense of tongues as the initial physical evidence of Spirit baptism. But as my dad writes, "We must not stop there."

He goes on: "We believe that baptism in the Spirit brings the delight of initially speaking with other tongues, but if we stop there, this Pentecostal experience will have no ongoing fruitfulness. I grew up in the Assemblies of God when it was preached that the baptism of the Spirit is for the *empowerment* of believers for life and service. . . . If we're not seeing this evidence— fruitfulness—we're in trouble." Authentic Pentecostalism involves both the *initial* and the *enduring* work of the Holy Spirit in the life of believers.

Authentic Pentecostalism is a restoration of New Testament Christianity. Is it possible that some in the Assemblies of God want to restore early-twentieth-century Pentecostalism rather than first-century Pentecostalism? Could they have confused biblical Pentecost with historical Pentecostalism?

"The idea of Pentecost," my dad writes in a different publication, "is to remove the accretive smudge of theological and experiential smoke and junk that has obscured what the church was at its beginning." Unless we are constantly reforming ourselves according to the biblical pattern of faith and works, we're not restoring anything but our own spiritual misconceptions. *Living in the Spirit* is a call to that kind of restoration.

At the Southern California District Council in 2008, my dad spoke on the theme, "And the Spirit said." This phrase is found four times in the Acts of the Apostles, and each time it occurs, the Spirit called believers out of themselves and into the world to proclaim and live out the gospel of Jesus Christ in the power of God. It was vintage dad: exegetical, practical and challenging. In fact, it was the best sermon I've ever heard my dad preach (and I've heard a lot of my dad's sermons).

What I most remember about that night is not my dad's sermon but his leadership in prayer. In many churches today, the prayer time is dominated by the endless repetition of simple worship songs at a loud volume. You walk away not knowing whether you met the Spirit or just got caught up in the frenzy. Dad turned to the worship team and politely asked them not to play. Then he turned to us and invited us to pray. We did, singing a cappella melodies of praise to our gracious God. And we felt the fruit of the Spirit growing up inside us as we did. It was a holy, life-changing moment. For me, that experience is the essence of Pentecostalism: holy and life-changing.

Pentecostalism is my heritage, just like the name George is. There are now four generations of *George Wood* in the Assemblies of God. There are at least as many generations of believers in our Movement. Without ever letting go of *George*, we should always make sure there's still room for *Reese*. In other words, without ever letting go of "the faith once delivered," we should always make room for the next generation. That twofold movement—of faithfulness to our heritage and openness to our future—is what *Living in the Spirit* is all about.

—GEORGE P. WOOD
Senior Pastor, Living Faith Center
Santa Barbara, California

WAS RECENTLY AT CHRIST GOSPEL CHURCH IN JEFFERSONVILLE, INDIANA—the successor to the failed church plant my parents tried to get going in the mid-1950s. The pastor, ninety-year-old Berniece Hicks, took over the building and the Lord has blessed her and the congregation. Today, Christ Gospel Church has about three thousand parishioners and has started more than two thousand churches worldwide.

Before the Sunday evening service, I noticed a thin trickle descending from top to bottom in the vision of my left eye. I knew this thin trickle could lead to a cascade of blood—the evidence of a significantly torn retina— because I'd experienced this before and had needed laser surgery to correct it.

The trickle continued through the service. After nearly everyone was gone, I called my secretary and asked her to make an eye appointment for me. I was flying back to Springfield early the next morning, and I hoped to get the problem taken care of as soon as possible.

Pastor Hicks and some of the elders had gathered in the office. When I stepped inside, I explained why I'd been on my cell phone. These people are all dear friends of mine, and one of the elders said, "Could we pray for you?"

I sat in a chair while the others gathered around me, laid hands on me, and prayed. When I opened my eyes at the end of the prayer, the trickle was totally gone.

The next morning I went to my ophthalmologist. After an examination, he told me there was no evidence of a tear or even a small hole in the retina. I knew I had been instantly healed the moment I opened my eyes after prayer.

Being Pentecostal means that we can expect divine intervention in our life at any moment. I was raised in a Pentecostal home in which we had a continual consciousness of and dependence on the Spirit's activity in our life.

Experiencing God's work in my life began very early, as I was saved at the age of ten. I dreamed one night that the Lord had returned and I wasn't ready. It was the middle of the night, and I was scared spitless that I had missed the Rapture. I wasn't sure if it was dream or if it had actually happened. I tiptoed to my parents' bedroom but I couldn't see them. I wasn't about to try to wake them up, because if they were there, they would wonder why I was troubled. If they weren't there, I didn't want to know—so I went back to bed and lay awake most of the night. I gave my life to the Lord that night.

It was from that point on that I began seeking the baptism in the Holy Spirit. But, unfortunately, I had a warped view of Spirit baptism. First, I had the idea that I needed to be unconscious to receive. Second, I was really afraid to receive. Having a quiet nature, people told me, "George, when you are baptized in the Spirit you are going to run, you are going to roll"—all the sorts of things that scared the life out of me. But, still I went down to the altar every service. Other kids received immediately. But, I'd still be trying. People would hold my hands up in the air, pat me on the back, and tell me to say things like "Glory, glory, glory, Hallelujah." I experienced this for six years.

After pioneering in Jeffersonville, Indiana, Dad felt led into evangelistic work and moved us to Springfield, Missouri, where we lived in a one-bedroom house near Central Bible College.

When I was fifteen, an evangelist named Bill Lewis came to Central Assembly in Springfield, where Mom and I attended, because Dad was on the road most of the time. Bill Lewis had a very calm nature but also an effective ministry of helping people receive the baptism in the Spirit. As I knelt at the altar one night and prayed, all of a sudden I found myself speaking in other tongues.

I had two instant reactions. One was the thought, *I'm conscious*, which was a surprise. Secondly, I realized that I had been praying this way in my spirit almost since my conversion, but I had never vocally expressed it because I thought I had to be in some sort of ecstatic state and people would wake me up after I received and tell me, "You got it!" This helped me better understand as an adult, Acts 2:4 "as the Spirit *gave them utterance*."[1] The Spirit gave, but they had to speak. That demystified Spirit baptism for me. It helped me understand that the Spirit wants us to pray in a language we have not learned right from the beginning, whether it is the language of men or the language of angels.

I felt that my praying in the Spirit, until that point in time, was inside me. I never allowed the Spirit to give articulation to my prayer—to receive and give release to the Spirit's fullness. The Spirit enters us at salvation and wants to baptize us—to overwhelm us with His presence and power. Jesus said that out of our "innermost being shall flow rivers of living waters."[2]

God knows what is in the heart and the Spirit intercedes for us according to the will of God. I'd made something difficult that should be so easy. Now, more than five decades later, every day, through praying in the Spirit, I enter dimensions beyond my cognitive being—to praise and intercede before the throne of God.

As wonderful as the Pentecostal experience is, we must still be vigilant in our spirituality and guard what God has entrusted to us. We must keep our relationship with the Holy Spirit fresh and our dependence on Him constant.

For my devotions this year, along with slowly moving through Ezekiel with Donald Bloch's terrific (and technical) commentary, I have been journaling through the Gospel of Mark. I've found this daily immersion in the Scripture to be really invigorating.

When I awakened one morning, I began to work my way through Mark 9 when suddenly some things fell together. Mark 9 reveals the disciples' perception of themselves and their place in the Kingdom. The chapter follows Jesus' disciples through four stages, in any of which we can find ourselves.

The first stage is *revelation*. That's the Transfiguration or "metamorphosis" of Jesus. It's the only time in His earthly life when His divine nature showed through His humanity. Moses and Elijah were present, Jesus' face is shining like the sun, and His clothes whiter than Clorox could get them. What an incredible moment for Peter, James and John.

Revelation is where we are overwhelmed in the presence of the majestic Christ. We Pentecostals covet being caught up into spiritual revelation and experience beyond what the rational mind can fathom—encountering God in such a way that language cannot adequately express the experience nor emotions be articulated.

The second stage is *argument*. When Jesus and three of His disciples came down from the mountain, they found the remaining nine disciples locked in an argument with the teachers of the Law. The disciples couldn't cast the demon out of the boy, even though Jesus had commissioned them earlier to cast out demons and they had done so. But, this day they commanded and nothing happened—so they're left to argue with the critics.

It seems to me that we have a similar problem now in the Pentecostal movement. When we don't have power, we tend to argue. But, our arguments don't solve the pressing needs of those who are looking to us. We have a dried-up Pentecostal theological scholasticism that has no power. Argument (other than a wholesome apologetic such as the apostle Paul's) produces neither the fruit nor the gifts of the Spirit.

At the foot of the Mount of Transfiguration, the powerless disciples could only fall back on defending themselves with argument. Jesus rebuked them for not praying, connecting argument with prayerlessness and authority with prayer.

The third stage is *arrogance*. After being reproved by Jesus for their powerlessness, they start arguing about who is the greatest. This breaks community. When we pit ourselves against others or take an "I don't need you" attitude, aren't we exhibiting the same kind of arrogance as the disciples?

So, Jesus set a little child in their midst and taught His disciples about being servants. I think what He told them is, "If you really want to be great, then put your arms around the next generation and serve them. My way is not self-fulfillment, but self-denial. My way is not independence, but interdependence."

Fortunately, by the time we get to the Book of Acts, the disciples have pretty much gotten over their arrogance and become an exemplary community. It took awhile for them to realize the world would know them, not by how smart they were, not by how cutting-edge they were, not by what their generational and cultural preferences were—but by their love for one another.

Then, a fourth stage happens. From revelation, to argument, to arrogance, they degenerate to *exclusionism*. When the disciples couldn't cast out the demon, they wanted other people who were casting out demons to stop. They thought they had the exclusive franchise on Jesus' ministry.

We must shrink from any narrowness of heart and spirit. Jesus told His disciples that they must not lead "little ones" into sin. If they did, it would be better if a millstone were tied around their neck. What He's really saying is that the fractiousness of the disciples will doom novices in the kingdom. This kind of exclusionism is not merely silly. It is spiritually deadly. I believe this passage of Scripture in Mark 9 is a telling example of the tendency we can have to degenerate in our spiritual focus and priorities.

In recent weeks, I've been asking the Lord to help me stay fresh on the revelation side so that I'm inundated with His presence and spared from becoming drawn into argumentation, arrogance or exclusionism.

For those who are ministers, it is not adequate to merely sign our credential renewal each year reaffirming our doctrines—and even to publicly proclaim them. We must see the Spirit's life and empowerment each day in our own life.

As you read the following chapters, I encourage you to have an open mind and heart to the Spirit's leading and moving in your life. When I so recently experienced His healing touch, it was a fresh confirmation of His presence and power.

May we all keep an ongoing, open connection—not a dial-up connection, but hardwired—to the lifeflow of the Spirit.

----

[1] KJV
[2] John 7:38, NASB

CHAPTER ONE

THE PERSON OF THE SPIRIT

I WILL PRAY *the*

FATHER, *and* HE

SHALL GIVE

YOU ANOTHER

COMFORTER, *that*

HE MAY ABIDE

WITH YOU FOREVER.

—John 14:16, KJV

A S A KID GROWING UP IN A PENTECOSTAL CHURCH, emphasis on the Holy Spirit sometimes filtered through to me in odd ways. I had a very difficult time relating to the Holy Spirit as a child and young person. I knew that Jesus loved me. But I felt the Holy Spirit didn't like me at all because He seemed to fill everyone but me.

His name didn't exactly ring a bell with me either, because He was often called the Holy *Ghost*. I was frightened of ghosts because they hung around dead people and they were spooky and mysterious. I didn't know the Holy Ghost—the Holy Spirit—as a loving Person who was already in my life and who was continually seeking to fill me more with the presence of God and make my personality like Jesus. So, I had a very warped view of the Holy Spirit.

When we ask the question, "Who is the Holy Spirit?" we recognize our limitations. God alone says, "I AM THAT I AM."[1] Only God can define himself and any of our attempts to describe God ultimately fall short. When we talk about the Person and character of God— God the Father, God the Son and God the Holy Spirit— we're trying to translate the understanding of God into our everyday experience and into language that can be appropriated.

But God has used human language in His Word to describe the Holy Spirit and we can at least get close using the language of Scripture to understand the Spirit.

THE PERSON OF THE SPIRIT

The first thing to note is that the Holy Spirit is a Person. When we talk about the Spirit, we are not talking about "the force." The Holy Spirit is different, for example, than a force such as electricity, which is nonpersonal in nature. This is a very critical perspective because the Holy Spirit is often thought of as being a power: He is powerful. But, He is a Person. If we simply think of Him as a power, then He becomes someone whom we try to get hold of and use. But because He is a Person, He is seeking to get hold of us and use us to bring glory to Christ.

Therefore, we ought to avoid referring to the Holy Spirit as "It," or describing the infilling of the Spirit in our life by saying, "We got It!" You will never find that kind of terminology used in the Bible. We don't so much get Him as He, the Holy Spirit, gets us. We, then, are delighted to receive His presence in ever-deepening dimensions in our life.

How do we know that the Holy Spirit is a Person? The Scriptures bear witness to this in a number of ways.

First, when the Holy Spirit is described, personal pronouns are used. In John 16, Jesus spoke of the coming of the Spirit that is to follow His ascension. He referred twelve times to the Holy Spirit with the masculine Greek pronoun, "He," specifically referring to the Spirit as a Person.

The Spirit is also personal in that He has a name, which Jesus used in John 14:16 when He said, "I will pray the Father, and he shall give you another Comforter."[2] There are two significant ideas concerning the use of the words *another* and *comforter* (or *paraclete*).

In the Greek language of Jesus' day, there were two words for *another*. One referred to another thing of a different kind—something totally unlike that which was first described. The other word was used to describe another of the same kind. When Jesus spoke of the Holy Spirit as being the Comforter, He was saying, "I'm going to send you another one like Me. Not someone different from Me, but another like Me." Jesus promised another Paraclete, which literally means, "one called alongside to help." The Holy Spirit is our personal Helper.

We know also from the Scripture that personal characteristics are given to the Holy Spirit. There are four essential elements of personality—intellect, feelings, will and actions. All of these are used to describe the Spirit.

Intellect: 1 Corinthians 2:11 says, "No one knows the thoughts of God except the Spirit of God." It takes a personality to know thoughts. For example, I've been behind my desk many times, but it does not know my thoughts, remember my thoughts, or have access to me, because it is inanimate. It is not living.

But the Holy Spirit is the living One who has access to the thoughts of God, even the deep things of God. Romans 8:27 says that the Holy Spirit also has access to us: "He who searches our heart knows the mind of the Spirit." The Spirit is the Person who has full access to all that is in God. He also has full access to all that is in me. Nothing in my life is unknown or inaccessible to the Holy Spirit.

Feelings: In Ephesians 4:30, we are told explicitly, "Do not grieve the Holy Spirit." The verse occurs in a context where various sins of the flesh are being described, including immorality and wrong language. Paul cautioned Christians that when we are tempted to act like the world and talk like the world, we must not give in because it grieves the Holy Spirit. When we are tempted to listen to or use language not fitting to that of Jesus, we immediately sense there is Someone present in our life who is not pleased with what is happening.

Will: First Corinthians 12:11 says that the Holy Spirit gives spiritual gifts to each as He wills. The gifts that are placed in the body of Christ and the assignment of responsibilities in the body of Christ come through the marvelous working of the Holy Spirit.

Actions: There is a long scriptural list of the Spirit's actions.

- He speaks. In Acts 13:2, the Spirit is the initiator of the first missionary journey of the church when He said, "Set apart for me Barnabas and Saul for the work to which I have called them."

- He testifies. He testifies concerning Jesus. The Spirit's function and His role is to bear witness to the living Lord.[3]

- He teaches. He teaches that which Jesus has taught. He brings to our remembrance the things the Lord has communicated to us. His fundamental role as Teacher is to make alive the person of Jesus in our life.[4]

- He convicts. The Spirit convicts of sin and of righteousness and of the judgment to come.[5]

- He intercedes for us. The Spirit is our Intercessor.[6]
  The Bible tells us we have an intercessor in the
  heavens—Jesus Christ—and we have in the heart the
  intercessor of the Holy Spirit. Whenever we're praying
  for ourself or other people are praying for us, we're
  never praying alone.

- He guides us into truth.[7] He directs our steps.[8] The
  Spirit did this with Paul, Silas and Timothy as they
  tried to go into an area of the world to preach the
  gospel where the Holy Spirit would not allow them.

- He reveals God's Word to us.[9] Prophecy, or the written
  Word of God, did not have its origin in men, but it was
  carried along to us and revealed to us by the Holy Spirit.

- He can be tested, as with Ananias and Sapphira who
  put Him to the test by being dishonest.[10]

- He can be lied to.[11] Peter said Ananias had lied to the
  Spirit in saying he was giving an offering, when he
  didn't give the complete offering.

- He can be grieved. We've already referred to Ephesians
  4:30. Isaiah 63:10 tells us, "Yet they rebelled and
  grieved his Holy Spirit. So he turned and became their
  enemy and he himself fought against them."

- He can be resisted. At the end of his great sermon,
  Stephen said to the people who were about to kill him,

"You always resist the Holy Spirit. As your fathers did, so do you."[12]

- He can be insulted[13] and He can be blasphemed. Jesus described the unforgivable sin as blasphemy against the Holy Spirit.[14] Blasphemy against the Holy Spirit is an absolute denial of what the Spirit is saying about Jesus. The Spirit is always saying to us, "Jesus is the Lord. He's the Son of God. Confess Him as Lord." At some point, when we continually resist the Spirit's testimony of Jesus, we blaspheme against the Spirit.

Since there is no forgiveness, Jesus said, either in this life or the age to come, for a person who blasphemes the Spirit, the subject of blasphemy against the Spirit is a separate topic. It is important to understand that any person who fears he or she has committed the unpardonable sin is still spiritually sensitive and has not committed that sin. Rather, the person who reaches this level of blasphemy no longer has any desire to receive God's grace and forgiveness because the Spirit no longer convicts that person's conscience of sin.

THE DIVINITY OF THE SPIRIT

The Holy Spirit is not merely a Person, He is a *divine* Person. The Spirit as a Person is in association and relationship with the Father and the Son. In Matthew 28:19, Jesus told His disciples to go everywhere, baptizing believers "in the name of the Father, and of the

Son and of the Holy Spirit." Notice how Jesus carefully forms the Trinitarian formula. He does not use the plural noun *names* as though Father, Son and Spirit were three different gods. Rather, there is one name of the one God who has revealed himself as Father, Son and Spirit. Second Corinthians 13:14 also shows the Spirit's association and relationship with the Father and the Son: "May the grace of the Lord Jesus Christ, and the love of God, and the fellowship of the Holy Spirit be with you all."

The Spirit bears the attributes of God.

- He is eternal. The writer to the Hebrews says, "How much more, then, will the blood of Christ, who through the eternal Spirit offered himself unblemished to God, cleanse our consciences from acts that lead to death, so that, we may serve the living God."[15] As it is said of Jesus—He is Alpha and Omega, the beginning and the end, so the Spirit has no origin and He has no ending.

- He is all-knowing. Jesus said, "The Holy Spirit, whom the Father will send in my name, will teach you all things and will remind you of everything I have said to you."[16]

John 16:12,13 speaks of the Spirit guiding us into all truth. "The Spirit searches all things, even the deep things of God. For who among men knows the thoughts of a man except the man's spirit within him? In the same way no one knows the thoughts of God except the Spirit of God."[17]

- He is all-powerful. The Spirit revealed this aspect of His nature to Mary through the angel Gabriel: "The Holy Spirit will come upon you, and the power of the Most High will overshadow you. So the holy one to be born will be called the Son of God. . . . For nothing is impossible with God."[18] The work of the Spirit in birthing Jesus in the womb of Mary is a mark of the omnipotence of the Spirit of God.

- He is present everywhere. Psalm 139:7–10 says, "Where can I go from your Spirit? Where can I flee from your presence? If I go up to the heavens, you are there; if I make my bed in the depths you are there. If I rise on the wings of the dawn, if I settle on the far side of the sea, even there your hand will guide me, your right hand will hold me fast."

The Spirit also does the works of God. We see the Spirit active in four key areas of God's activity.

- First, He is involved in creation. Genesis 1:2 says, "The earth was without form, and void; and darkness was upon the face of the deep. And the spirit of God moved upon the face of the waters."[19] The New International Version says, "the Spirit of God was hovering over the waters."

That is such an eloquent introduction in Scripture to the divine personality of the Spirit, who brings creation out of chaos. I would suggest to you that this also describes the work of the Spirit in your life and mine. Our life without God is chaos. The Spirit of God wants to create in us the personality of Jesus and to breathe into the formlessness and the void of our life the life of Jesus. The Spirit is at work in that creation process. It is part of His divine nature.

• Second, He is involved in regeneration. "When you send your Spirit, they are created, and you renew the face of the earth."[20] As the Spirit brooded over the material creation of the earth and brought everything into being through His creative act, He is also at work in the spiritual re-creation of our inner life.

"I will give you a new heart and put a new spirit in you; I will remove from you your heart of stone and give you a heart of flesh. And I will put my Spirit in you and move you to follow my decrees and be careful to keep my laws."[21] John 3:5,6 reemphasizes a new heart made by the Spirit when Jesus said, "No one can enter the Kingdom of God unless he is born of water and the Spirit. Flesh gives birth to flesh, but the Spirit gives birth to spirit." The Spirit is always seeking to birth us into the kingdom of God.

Jesus does a beautiful thing in putting together the Spirit's work in creation with the Spirit's work in the human personality. After Christ's resurrection, He appears to His disciples and speaks peace to them. Then the Scripture says, "With that he breathed on them and said, 'Receive the Holy Spirit.'"[22] Even as God breathed life into the lifeless form of man at creation, so Jesus spoke to His disciples and breathed into them life which is eternal.

• Third, the Spirit is active in giving us the Scriptures. "All Scripture is God-breathed."[23] The King James Version says, "All Scripture is inspired." The correct translation of the Greek word is, "All Scripture is expired," that is, *breathed out*. All Scripture is the product of the breath of God. The function of the Spirit is to breathe the presence of God into human life. The Bible is a result of the activity of the wind of the Spirit—God breathing His word out of His nature.

• Fourth, the Spirit is involved in resurrection from death. "And if the Spirit of him who raised Jesus from the dead is living in you, he who raised Christ from the dead will also give life to your mortal bodies through his Spirit, who lives in you."[24] The Spirit is the agent transferring the eternal life of God to us. The Spirit who raised Jesus from the dead lives also in you and me.

SYMBOLS OF THE SPIRIT

The Person of the Spirit is further revealed to us through symbols.

• The first is wind. The very idea of spirit is associated with the words *wind* or *breath*. The Hebrew word is *ruach*, which is translated as the English word *spirit*.

When you find the name of the Spirit in the Old Testament, it is as wind or breath, the same word used in other contexts for those terms. In the Greek, the word for *spirit* is *pneuma*—or filled with air, wind or breath.

The Spirit therefore reflects that invisible essential in the life of God. Unlike people who have bodies, the Spirit of God does not have a body. Yet His personality is very much seen. If you want to know a person, you have to know that person's spirit. A body never tells you who that person is. God exists without a body (except in the incarnation of Jesus) and yet is a Person. The Spirit's personality is represented to us by wind or breath, which is everywhere present and essential for life. There is no life without breath. The Spirit, described as wind, is communicating to us the eternal life of God which is breathed upon us.

• Second, the Spirit is represented as water. In John 7:37,38, on the last day of the Feast of Tabernacles, Jesus stood up and said, "If anyone is thirsty, let him come to me and drink. Whoever believes in me, as the Scripture has said, streams of living water will flow from within him." You'll be like an artesian well. "By this he meant the Spirit, whom those who believed in him were later to receive."[25]

What is the nature of water? We know water is essential to life. We know water washes and refreshes. The Spirit is described as water so that we might also know He is essential to our life. He is the refreshing agent of God to our personalities and He fills us with joy and power. He is also at work washing us, convicting us of our sin, and administering the cleansing life of Jesus to us.

• A third sign or symbol of the Spirit is that of a seal pressed upon a letter or document. "And you also were included in Christ when you heard the word of truth, the gospel of your salvation. Having believed, you were marked in him with a seal, the promised Holy Spirit."[26] When you became a Christian, God put the stamp of His ownership upon your life. It was the Holy Spirit that God placed upon your life as the mark that He owns you.

A seal is both a sign of ownership and a mark of authenticity. In ancient days, a document's authenticity was based on matching the known seal. Likewise, the Spirit impresses upon our life. He marks us as being owned by God and that our lives are authentically controlled by God.

• Fourth, the Spirit is represented by oil. Jesus said, "The Spirit of the Lord is on me because he has anointed me [placed oil upon me] to preach good news."[27] The Spirit comes upon us to show that He wants to especially empower us to do the work that Christ has called us to do. The mark of that empowerment and anointing is symbolized by oil. In the Old Testament, no king began his administration without being anointed with oil. It was a mark that prophetic approval had been given for him to function as king. No high priest began his ministry without first being anointed with oil. The prophets also began their ministry by being anointed with oil.

It's not surprising when we open the Book of Acts that before the Church began, the Holy Spirit came upon the Church to equip it and get its ministry underway. The Spirit wants to come upon us in the same way, designating us as His ambassadors in the world.

• Fifth, the Spirit is represented by the sign of the dove. The Holy Spirit descended on Jesus "in bodily form like a dove."[28] A dove testifies to gentleness, tenderness and, of course, it is the universal sign of peace. The Holy Spirit being represented as a dove means that He does not come to us represented in a violent figure. It's important to realize that the Holy Spirit, like Jesus, waits for us to unlock the door of our life and let Him into our personality. He does not force His way into our life. He comes gently, tenderly and peacefully.

EXPERIENCING THE SPIRIT

It is never sufficient to simply describe the Holy Spirit; we need to experience the Spirit. The Spirit will never be known simply by reading about Him. The Spirit will only be known as we call upon Him to indwell our life and empower our life. The church can't operate without the Spirit. You can have programs and printed bulletins; you can have organization, boards and committees. But the church cannot function without the Holy Spirit. And our personal life cannot function without the Holy Spirit. We might know a lot about theology. We might study our Bible on a regular basis. But unless we have the operating presence of the Spirit in our life, we are not doing anything that really counts in the kingdom of God.

I want to close by noting four things in the Book of Acts about the Spirit in our experience—what the Spirit is doing when He comes upon us.

• First, the Holy Spirit creates unity among us without producing uniformity. When the Spirit of God enters us, we do not become clones. In fact, the Scriptures say that the Spirit places great variety in the body of Christ—varieties of ministry, personality, ministerial office, all flowing out of the one Spirit. The Spirit ministers to us the life of Jesus, which is the source of our unity, but He also brings us into conformity with Christlikeness without making us "cookies" cut from the same mold. The Spirit creates unity without uniformity.

• Second, the Spirit taps the potential in our life that no one or nothing else can reach. No single person's life is ever the same after having encountered the Holy Spirit. No person in the New Testament would have ever expressed the potential in his or her life unless the Holy Spirit had been upon them. No matter what our talents and personality are, no matter how much energy we bring to any particular assignment or task, only the Holy Spirit can touch the depths of potential in our life and draw them forth for the kingdom of God.

I feel, at this moment in my life, that I need the Holy Spirit more than I have ever needed Him before. I want a fresh anointing of the Spirit. I want a fresh filling of the Spirit. I realize that I haven't been filled enough with the Spirit. I believe the New Testament reveals, in regard to the infilling of the Spirit, that we are expansible. He is infinite and is capable of giving more, and we are capable of receiving more. I'll never realize the potential God has for my life unless the Spirit fills me, unless I open myself to let Him touch the potential in my life.

- Third, the Spirit is always leading us in two dimensions simultaneously. He's always leading us deeper into God and He's always leading us out into the world. The Spirit's desire is to make us more spiritual, more godly, more like Jesus. He wants to lead us deeper into God. We need to be careful how we define the deeper things of God. The deeper things of God move us to love as God loves and to experience His purity and joy. The deeper things of God are not about spooky spirituality or being smarter or holier than the next person. The deeper things of God are meant to impress our life more dramatically with the personality of God through Christ Jesus.

At the same time, the Spirit leads us out into the world, because God loves the world. The Father gave His Son to save the world. Jesus told us to go into the world, but He said we can't go into the world unless the Spirit comes upon us. He told the disciples to wait until the Spirit did that. The Spirit is always pulling us deeper into God and more thoroughly into ministry to a lost world.

We see this in the Old Testament with Isaiah. In Isaiah 6:1, the prophet was worshipping the Lord and said, "I saw the Lord seated on a throne, high and exalted, and the train of his robe filled the temple." Isaiah was lost in worship to God and the next thing he knew, God said, "Whom shall I send? And who will go for us?"[29] Caught up in adoration of God, Isaiah heard God say, "I've got a work for you to do." When you worship God, He will point you to His work and where it is, in your family, in the church, and in the world.

- Fourth, the Holy Spirit is indeed a Person and as such, you can resist Him, ignore Him or welcome Him. He waits to be received; He waits to be invited. Jesus said to ask the Father and He will give you the Holy Spirit.[30] The Spirit will not storm down the door of our life. He seeks an invitation. We ask, seek and knock and welcome the Spirit.

Pentecostals are very good about asking, "Are you filled with the Spirit?" However, that immediately makes some people defensive. "Of course, I am filled with the

Spirit. I spoke in tongues thirty years ago! Why would you ask me that question?" There are others who will answer, "Of course, I am filled with the Spirit. I hope you're not talking about tongues. Because when I gave my life to Jesus, I was filled with the Spirit."

If you read the Book of Acts carefully, you discover that time and again in the life of Jesus' disciples, at critical junctures in their lives the text says, "They were filled with the Spirit." That filling of the Spirit is a post-Pentecost filling. It is not the filling of Acts 2; it is a filling subsequent to that. The Spirit continued to fill the disciples at moments when they faced challenges they had never faced before, when a new level of power was called for in their personality that they had never needed before. With each new challenge comes a new demand for a fresh filling of the Spirit.

This must be our experience of the Spirit today. It is not simply that the Spirit came upon us when we were baptized in the Spirit. The Spirit, in our present challenges, is filling us to every level of capacity. May we be filled at this moment in life with all of God that we can take. May we experience to the deepest level and core of our being the fullness of God that the Spirit makes present!

---

[1] Exodus 3:14, KJV

[2] KJV

[3] John 15:26

[4] John 14:26

[5] John 16:8–11

[6] Romans 8:26,27

[7] John 16:13

[8] Acts 16:6,7

[9] 2 Peter 1:21

[10] Acts 5:9

[11] Acts 5:3

[12] Acts 7:51, ESV

[13] Hebrews 10:29

[14] Matthew 12:31,32

[15] Hebrews 9:14

[16] John 14:26

[17] 1 Corinthians 2:10,11

[18] Luke 1:35,37

[19] KJV

[20] Psalm 104:30

[21] Ezekiel 36:26,27

[22] John 20:21,22

[23] 2 Timothy 3:16

[24] Romans 8:11

[25] 7:39

[26] Ephesians 1:13

[27] Luke 4:18

[28] Luke 3:22

[29] 6:8

[30] Luke 11:13

CHAPTER TWO

THE BAPTISM AND FULLNESS OF THE SPIRIT

IN *the* LAST DAYS,
GOD SAYS, I WILL
POUR OUT MY
SPIRIT *on* ALL PEOPLE.
YOUR SONS *and*
DAUGHTERS WILL
PROPHESY, YOUR
YOUNG MEN WILL
SEE VISIONS, YOUR
OLD MEN WILL
DREAM DREAMS.

—Acts 2:17

I HAVE BEEN ASKED A NUMBER OF TIMES BY NATIONAL REPORTERS ABOUT SPEAKING IN TONGUES. I was talking with a reporter from the *New York Times* and told him there's nothing unusual about what Pentecostals are doing today. If you look at the first-century church, all the writers of the New Testament spoke in tongues and the Early Church spoke in tongues. So Pentecostalism, at its roots, is basically a restorationist movement. We believe that we can cut through twenty centuries of church tradition and get back to the original church. It doesn't mean that we do everything like the original church, but we're trying to have the same doctrine and experience of the Early Church.

Several decades ago, I visited the Sistine Chapel in Rome. Looking up to Michelangelo's great fresco of *The Last Judgment*, I thought to myself, *Why is everyone raving about this work of art?* It's very occluded and dark. What had happened is that over the last four centuries, there have been so many candles burning in the Sistine Chapel that the smoke had gradually put a layer of gray over the painting. So when I saw how dark it was, I wasn't impressed at all. Now, many years later, it has been restored. All the smudge is gone and the colors are radiant and alive, and it's as though the painting had just been done yesterday. That's what Pentecostalism, in its purist form, tries to do. It tries to erase the smudges on the church for the last twenty centuries and get back to what the early Christians believed and practiced. That is our goal—to get back to biblical, original Christianity.

Three primary views within the church describe the baptism in the Holy Spirit. One is the view that the baptism in the Holy Spirit and any terminology connected with it in Scripture are meant to be taken as synonymous with conversion—that when we give our life to the Lord we are automatically baptized in the Spirit.

In this view, the Day of Pentecost in Acts 2 represents the moment the members of the Early Church became Christians. The baptism in the Holy Spirit, therefore, is not meant to be repeated in believers' lives today in the manner described in Acts 2, 8, 9, 10 and 19, but is to be seen as God's way of giving the Church a giant cosmic shove into its centuries of existence.

On the opposite extreme are those who treat the baptism in the Holy Spirit as the highest goal of Christian experience—a goal that once reached need not be sought after again. Unfortunately, this is the view I had of the baptism in the Spirit while I was a child and teenager. In a particular church of which I was a part, you couldn't hold office in the youth group unless you had been baptized in the Spirit. So, Spirit baptism was the highest goal of my life. Consequently, when I received it, I promptly relaxed.

> Spirit baptism was the highest goal of my life. Consequently, when I received it, I promptly relaxed.

Only years later did I come to fully realize the function of the baptism in the Spirit. This, I believe, is the third view. Spirit baptism is a distinct part of our entrance into the full Christian life, along with salvation and water baptism. These can each occur at different times, but I believe it is God's purpose to make this a cluster of initiation events into the Christian life.

Those who believe the baptism in the Spirit is part of our initiation into the Christian life are called Pentecostal or charismatic. I favor the term *Pentecostal* primarily because it seems a more biblical word to describe the experience. Whereas *charismatic* is not used in the Book of Acts and generally refers to spiritual gifts, the *charismata* in general.

The focus of the baptism in the Spirit is twofold. It deepens our worship of the Lord through giving us a language of praise that we have not learned—speaking with other tongues. It also gives us power in our Christian witness. I'd like to explore five scriptural terms used of the Baptism.

BAPTISM IN THE SPIRIT

The first term is the "baptism *in* the Spirit." Anyone who has translated a language knows that prepositions are very difficult to use in any language. In English, for example, we have the prepositions "in" and "by." For the Greeks, the preposition *en* could refer to "in," "by" or even "with."

The term "baptism *in* the Spirit" occurs twice in the Book of Acts—both spoken by Jesus. In Acts 1:5, Jesus said, "For John baptized with water, but in a few days you will be baptized *with* the Holy Spirit." Then, in Acts 11:16, after Cornelius's Spirit baptism, Peter said, "Then I remembered what the Lord had said, 'John baptized with water but you will be baptized *with* the Holy Spirit.'" In both Acts 1 and Acts 11, though most translations including the NIV and NASB refer to baptism *with* the Holy Spirit, in each case the word translated as *with* is the Greek word *en*.

Note the sequence of how this term is used. It is used by the Lord after the experience of John 20:22. On the first evening after His resurrection, Jesus appeared to His disciples behind closed doors and breathed upon them and said, "Receive the Holy Spirit." This was the moment that the fruit of Christ's victory in the Cross and in the Resurrection was realized by the disciples. Until that time, their faith had only been the faith of every Old Testament person—the faith that anticipated what God would someday do. Now, all the benefits that could be won by Christ had been won. Through the Spirit, His eternal life was breathed into the disciples.

Therefore, it is appropriate to say that when we have received Christ, we have received the Spirit. The Pentecostal message is greatly misunderstood if anyone assumes that someone who has not received the baptism in the Spirit has not received the Person of the Spirit in conversion. We all receive the Spirit of God in conversion. No one can call Christ Lord except by the Spirit. When you and I became Christians, we didn't become "two-thirds Christians" having only the Father and Son's presence. We have the Father, Son and Holy Spirit.

> It is appropriate to say that when we have received Christ, we have received the Spirit.

When Jesus talked in Acts 1:5 and when He is quoted in Acts 11:16, He is speaking about the Holy

Spirit's work. But He speaks about it in a different context than that of John 20:22, since He is talking to people who had already received the Spirit. He's saying to them, "In a few days, you will be baptized *in* the Holy Spirit."

Some Christians try to generalize the Baptism by citing 1 Corinthians 12:13: "For we were all baptized by one Spirit into one body—whether Jews or Greeks, slave or free—and we were all given the one Spirit to drink." They say, "Here it is, as plain as plain as can be! All Christians have been baptized by the Spirit. The baptism in the Spirit subsequent to conversion is not a scriptural teaching."

This particular view has two problems. It fails to understand the difference between the Holy Spirit's work in John 20:22 and that promised by Jesus in Acts 1:5. It also fails to understand the different ways in which the Holy Spirit is at work. This may hang partly on the understanding of the preposition *en*, which can mean "with," "by means of," or simply "in."

We are either baptized *by* the Spirit or we are baptized *in* the Spirit. Paul said in 1 Corinthians 12 that "by the Spirit we were all baptized into Christ." Jesus said, on the other hand, that we are to be baptized *in* the Spirit. Can it be that the same preposition has two different meanings? Let me suggest to you that it does.

Consider, for example, Matthew 3:11. John the Baptist said, "I indeed baptize you with water . . . he shall baptize you *with* the Holy Spirit."[1] As in the two instances cited in Acts, the text in Matthew 3 quoting John the Baptist uses the Greek word *en* and is translated in most versions as *with*. In other words John was saying,

"The same way I baptize you in water will be the way He baptizes you in the Spirit." Did John baptize *by means of* water or *in* the water? If he baptized *by means of* water, it could have meant he took some water and placed it upon the candidate. If he baptized *in* the water, it meant he submerged the person in the water. We know from Scripture how John baptized. Matthew 3:16 tells us Jesus came up out of the water. When the preposition *out* is used, it means He was in it. John 3:23 says John was baptizing in a certain place because many waters were there. The Greek uses the plural of *water* for water in a river, so the depth of the water is indicated. Had he not baptized *in* water he wouldn't need much water.

Therefore, water baptism means to be baptized *in* water, not simply baptized *by means of* water. Baptism itself in the Greek language meant "to immerse." The Greeks used it in reference to the sinking of ships—submerged in the water. They used it of crowds overwhelming a city. Therefore, the baptism in the Spirit means to be immersed, to be sunk, to be overwhelmed in the environment or the person of the Spirit. John baptized in water. Jesus baptizes in the Spirit.[2]

> ...the baptism in the Spirit means to be immersed, to be sunk, to be overwhelmed in the environment or the person of the Spirit.

Essentially, there are three baptisms in Scripture: (1) the baptism into the body of Christ by the Spirit, which is conversion; (2) water baptism; and, (3) the baptism in the Spirit, which is the Pentecost experience. When we are converted, the agent of the conversion is the Spirit, who places us into the body of Christ. This is conversion. In water baptism, the agent of the baptism is the minister. This act follows conversion. In the Pentecostal experience of Acts 2, the agent of baptism is not the minister or the Spirit, but Christ, who is the Baptizer. The element into which we are placed is the Spirit and this occurs either alongside conversion or after conversion. In conversion, the Spirit acts as the agent ushering us into the life of Christ. In the baptism in the Spirit, Jesus is the agent who ushers us into the dimension of the fullness of the Spirit.

THE THREE BAPTISMS *in the* NEW TESTAMENT			
	BAPTISM INTO CHRIST (1 Cor. 12:13)	BAPTISM IN THE SPIRIT (Acts 2:4)	BAPTISM IN WATER (Acts 2:38-41)
AGENT of the BAPTISM (the Baptizer)	The Holy Spirit	Christ	The Minister
CANDIDATE	The Believer	The Believer	The Believer
ELEMENT INTO WHICH the CANDIDATE IS PLACED	Christ	The Holy Spirit	Water

Jesus' earthly experience with the Spirit is a model for our own. Jesus was conceived by the Spirit. Yet, at His baptism, the Spirit came upon Him like a dove. That He was conceived of the Spirit meant that all through His existence the Spirit resided in Him. Yet, as He began His earthly ministry, the Spirit came upon Him. This does not mean that until that time the Spirit was absent from Him. It meant Jesus' public ministry had begun and He needed the Spirit's empowerment. That's why after the temptation in the wilderness He could say, "The Spirit of the Lord is upon me."[3] The Spirit had always been in

Him, but at His baptism there was a necessary experience of the Spirit coming upon Him.

The Church models that same experience of the Spirit. We are conceived by the Spirit. The life of Jesus is born into us; we are born of the Spirit. Everyone who has Jesus has the Spirit living in him or her. But there is a subsequent work we find in Acts 2, when believers assumed their spiritual responsibilities. For this, we need the Spirit to come upon us. We need to be placed into the Spirit even as the Spirit has placed us into Christ.

THE PROMISE OF THE FATHER

A second term used to describe the baptism in the Spirit is "the promise of the Father." In Luke 24:49, Jesus states, "I am going to send you what my Father has promised; but stay in the city until you have been clothed with power from on high." Again, this followed the events of John 20:22, when He breathed upon them saying, "Receive the Spirit." Jesus was telling believers who already had the Spirit of God living in them, "Don't go out and do your work until the Spirit of God comes upon you. You're going to receive the promise of the Father."

In Acts 1:4,5, Jesus said again, "Do not leave Jerusalem, but wait for the gift my Father promised, which you have heard me speak about. For John baptized with water, but in a few days you will be baptized with the Holy Spirit."

Acts 2:1–4 tells us that this promise came to pass. On the Day of Pentecost, the Spirit came upon the 120 believers. In fact, He is described as being outpoured or

THE BAPTISM AND FULLNESS OF THE SPIRIT • 57

THE BAPTISM AND FULLNESS OF THE SPIRIT • 57

even falling upon them. Peter, in his sermon, described the promise: "Exalted to the right hand of God, he has received from the Father the promised Holy Spirit and has poured out what you now see and hear."[4] Note the promise is something seen and heard.

The crowds saw a group of people praising the Lord in all the languages spoken in the Near East. Acts 2:4 says this crowd of 120 were speaking in other tongues "as the Spirit gave them utterance."[5] The New International Version weakens the strong Greek verb here and says simply, "They spoke in other tongues as the Spirit enabled them." The force of the original says the Spirit "gave them to utter." *Utterance* is a key word to this promise. What they uttered, according to Acts 2:11, were the wonders of God in tongues they had never learned.

Wonders is a word that means magnificent, splendor, grand, great, sublime, beautiful, mighty. People saw the 120 and heard them talking about the magnificence, the splendor, the grandness, the greatness, the sublimity, the beauty and the mighty deeds of God. They were describing how powerful and wonderful God is. In Scripture, the word *utter* means "to speak out loudly and clearly." There is an emphasis upon enthusiasm. Enthusiasm means to be "in God." When the Old Testament used the verb *utter*, it referred to prophetic speech. "David, together with the commanders of the army, set apart some of the sons of Asaph, Heman and Jeduthun for the

In Scripture, the word *utter* means "to speak out loudly and clearly." There is an emphasis upon enthusiasm. Enthusiasm means to be "in God."

ministry of prophesying [utterance], accompanied by
harps, lyres and cymbals."[6]

The verb *utter* is used in Acts 2:14 when Peter began
to speak to the crowd. The English translation says he
"raised his voice and addressed the crowd,"[7] but the Greek says, "He uttered to the crowd." The same word used in Acts 2:4 is used in 2:14. Peter was declaring loudly and forcibly the claims of Jesus. In Acts 26:25, *utter* occurs once more. It does not mean "reply," as the New International Version has it, but

> We don't gradually conjure up the Spirit of ecstasy or knock ourselves out in spiritual therapy trying to get the Spirit.

rather, as Festus interrupted Paul's defense, Paul responded
to him in very clear articulation—enthused speech.

The promise of the Father is something seen and
heard, something that gave the disciples power to utter
boldly how great God is, to praise Him unashamedly,
and after praising Him, to go out and utter strongly and
powerfully as a witness. As believers, it can be difficult
for us to boldly and unashamedly praise God and clearly
and carefully set forth the claims of Jesus Christ in
witnessing. The promise of the Father comes upon us so
that we might have the power of utterance that magnifi-
cently declares God's glory and greatness.

Acts 2:17 says that Joel's words of the promise were
being fulfilled. The promise of the Father was not just to
launch the Church. Peter said to the crowd in Acts
2:38,39:

> Repent and be baptized, every one of you, in the
> name of Jesus Christ for the forgiveness of your

sins. And you will receive the gift of the Holy Spirit. The promise is for you and your children and for all who are far off—for all whom the Lord our God will call.

What is the promise? Whom is it for? Just for the 120? Just for the Day of Pentecost? The promise the Lord gave, the promise that can be seen and heard is for those who are afar off. It is for us today.

GIFT OF THE SPIRIT

The third term for the baptism in the Spirit used in the Book of Acts simply says to receive "the gift of the Spirit." When referred to in Acts, the word *charisma* is not used but the other Greek word, which means "a gift without payment" is. We don't earn it. We don't work for it. We don't gradually conjure up the Spirit of ecstasy or knock ourselves out in spiritual therapy trying to get the Spirit. The Spirit is a gift.

In Acts 2:38, Peter declared, "You will receive the gift of the Holy Spirit." He was talking about the same thing that the crowds had just witnessed among the 120—the promise of the Father.

In Acts 8:18–20, Simon wanted to buy the gift of the Spirit of God with money. What he wanted to buy was that which the disciples in Samaria had received when the Holy Spirit was given by the laying on of the apostles' hands.

Acts 10:45,46 says, "The circumcised believers who had come with Peter were astonished that the gift of the Holy Spirit had been poured out even on the Gentiles.

For they heard them speaking in tongues and praising God." Here's a very clear and explicit reference to the fact that the baptism in the Spirit is synonymous with receiving the gift of the Spirit.

In Acts 11:17, Peter said, "So if God gave them the same gift as he gave us, who believed in the Lord Jesus Christ, who was I to think that I could oppose God?"

RECEIVING THE SPIRIT

The fourth term for the baptism in the Spirit is simply to receive the Spirit. The expression "receive the Spirit" can be used in more than one sense. It's obvious from John 20:22 that we all receive the Spirit at conversion. Therefore, when we read Acts 8:15–17, we find believers in Samaria who had already put their faith in the Lord Jesus Christ. Many of them had been healed. They were devout Christians by that time. But when Peter and John arrived, "they prayed for them that they might receive the Holy Spirit." Certainly, they had already received the Spirit in the sense of conversion. In fact, they'd even been baptized in water. But now, Peter and John prayed that they might receive the Spirit because the Spirit had not fallen or come upon them. When Peter and John placed their hands upon the Samaritans, they received the Holy Spirit.

In Acts 19:2, Paul came to a small band of followers of John the Baptist and said to them, "Have ye received the Holy Ghost since ye believed?"[8] Some translate this as, "*When* you believed did you receive the Spirit?" Or, "*Since* you believed did you receive the Spirit?" Should we translate it, "*Since* you believed" or "*When* you believed"? There are some who say Paul is obviously saying "*When* you believed, did you receive the Spirit," because every believer receives the Spirit at conversion. Most Pentecostals say it means "*Since* you believed, did you receive the Spirit" because we receive the Spirit after we believe.

Fortunately we have some guidance from the Scripture on this. The actions are not identical, although some may think they are. Two instances in Acts illustrate the difference. When you have the phrase, "Have ye received the Holy Ghost since ye believed," at Samaria the answer would have been, "No, we did not receive the Spirit." But if you had asked at Cornelius's house, "Have ye received the Holy Ghost since ye believed," their answer would be yes, since they received the Spirit simultaneously with conversion.

Pentecostals have gotten in trouble when they carelessly infer to other believers that you have not received the Spirit if you have not received the baptism in the Spirit. That is not the case. The word *received* is used precisely in Acts to describe the baptism in the Spirit. But in John 20 it is used precisely to describe conversion.

FILLED WITH THE SPIRIT

This leads us to the fifth term, which is "filled with the Spirit." On the Day of Pentecost, "All of them were filled with the Holy Spirit."[9] This occurs subsequent to John 20:22. *Filled*, in this case, is the past tense verb, which means that the point is fixed in time and has happened.

This is not the only time, however, that the expression "filled with the Spirit" is used in the Book of Acts.

"After they prayed, the place where they were meeting was shaken. And they were all filled with the Holy Spirit and spoke the word of God boldly."[10] This is different from Acts 2:4. In Acts 4, the church was facing persecution for the first time. They needed more of God than they had ever received of Him before. So, those who had been filled with the Spirit in Acts 2 are described as again being filled with the Spirit in Acts 4. We should never take a view of the Holy Spirit that once we are baptized in the Spirit we have all that He offers. While there is one baptism, there are many fillings of the Spirit.

> Our filling is dependent on our capacity and each person has a different level of capacity. What is a "filling" for me may be only a thimbleful for you.

Consider Acts 9:17: "Then Ananias went to the house and entered it. Placing his hands on Saul, he said, 'Brother Saul, the Lord—Jesus, who appeared to you on the road as you were coming here—has sent me so that you may see again and be filled with the Holy Spirit.'" Ananias was talking to a man who had already been converted.

When we speak of the filling of the Spirit as it is associated with the baptism in the Spirit, we make a mistake if we compare our filling to another person's. Our filling is dependent on our capacity and each person has a different level of capacity. What is a "filling" for me may be only a thimbleful for you. Your capacity of being filled with all the fullness of God in terms of expressing gifted-ness of the Spirit may be far greater than mine. They were all filled on the Day of Pentecost, but only one person got up out of the 120 and preached a sermon and saw three thousand people converted. The disciples were capable of receiving more of the Spirit and He was capable of giving more of himself.

When you come to the words "filled with the Spirit" in the latter part of Acts, you will always find it associated with crises. Stephen was "full of the Spirit"[11] when he was selected as a deacon. When he later confronted those who were going to stone him to death, Acts 7:55 says he was "full of the Holy Spirit." Does this mean until that time in Stephen's life he hadn't been filled with the Spirit? Not at all. He was filled with the Spirit when he was chosen as a deacon. He was filled with the Spirit when he was baptized in the Spirit. But as he faced his own death, he needed new strength from God. So again, the Scripture says he was full of the Spirit.

The same phrase is used of Paul in Acts 13:9, when he meets the magician, Bar-Jesus, who tries to withstand his gospel witness. Paul, full of the Spirit, looked at him and brought blindness upon him. Paul had never faced a situation like that before, and he needed the Spirit in a new measure.

I would suggest, from a scriptural point of view, the appropriate question is not "Did you receive the Spirit?" but "Are you filled with the Spirit?" We don't earn the baptism in the Spirit like a merit badge and say, "I got it!" There are always new demands, new emergencies and new needs in life. We need the fullness of God's Spirit *today*.

INITIAL EVIDENCE AND EXPERIENCE

We have often been criticized by our non-Pentecostal friends for two things: taking our doctrine of Spirit baptism from a narrative portion of Scripture (the Book of Acts) and basing our position on Spirit baptism on our own experience and then hunting in Scripture for proof texts to back us up. The clearest examples of building doctrine from narrative Scripture are the teachings of both the virgin birth and the Trinity. No mention of the virgin birth is made in the didactic portions (epistles) of the New Testament; and the clearest setting forth of the Trinity is the record of Jesus' baptism—in which the Son is baptized, the Spirit descends, and the Father speaks.

"In the last days, God says, I will pour out my Spirit on all people." The idea of the pouring of the Spirit is that we get thoroughly soaked in the Spirit's presence.

I'll leave it to others to more thoroughly explore this subject, but I want to demonstrate briefly that basing doctrine on narrative Scripture (Matthew, Mark, Luke, John and Acts) is a valid hermeneutical practice.

The criticism of building doctrine from experience needs a response.

We understand that Spirit baptism comes in two ways. First, we set forth the pattern of Scripture as found in Acts 2, 8, 9, 10 and 19. That's what happened on January 1, 1901 in Topeka, Kansas. Charles Parham's Bible school students had been intentionally studying the Book of Acts and came to the conclusion that tongues are the initial physical evidence of Spirit baptism. The teaching led to their expecting and receiving the Spirit.

Second, Pentecostal history is replete with those upon whom the Spirit has fallen and who did not have a prior expectation of what would happen. That certainly was the case in Acts 2. But, immediately after receiving the gift of the Spirit, Peter announced the biblical basis for the experience: "This is what was spoken by the prophet Joel: 'In the last days, God says, I will pour out my Spirit on all people. Your sons and daughters will prophesy, your young men will see visions.'"[12]

Peter immediately went to the Scripture to corroborate the experience. We do the same thing. The experience of Spirit baptism and the doctrine supporting Spirit baptism with the initial physical evidence of speaking in other tongues are inseparable. You can't have one without the other, but there is always a sure biblical foundation for our experience—whether the experience precedes our understanding or our understanding ushers us into the experience.

For Pentecostals, our experience of Spirit baptism vivifies the Scripture. Our experience has brought what the text teaches to life.

FLOODS OF BLESSING

It's interesting that the baptism in the Spirit has three beautiful words to describe what the Spirit does for us. The words are all associated with water. Acts 2:17 says that the Spirit of God is *outpoured*: "In the last days, God says, I will pour out my Spirit on all people." The idea of the pouring of the Spirit is that we get thoroughly soaked in the Spirit's presence.

Acts 1:5 tells us that we will be baptized in the Spirit. This means we will be overwhelmed or *immersed* in the Spirit's presence. The expression "baptism in the Spirit" can have too narrow a meaning to us; we don't think of it in a fresh way. I want to ask in my own life, "Have I been overwhelmed by the Spirit? Am I soaked in the Spirit?"

Acts 2:4 uses another word associated with water: *filled* with the Spirit. When the Spirit is poured out upon us, it is the external coming of the Spirit *upon* us. When we are baptized in the Spirit, it is us *in* the Spirit. When we are filled with the Spirit, it is the Spirit *in* us. Furthermore, 1 Corinthians 12:13 says, "We were all given the one Spirit to drink." John 7:37–39 says we will have the Spirit of God welling up within us, flowing out of us—streams of living water.

Is the term "baptism in the Spirit" scriptural? Yes, it is. It is used by the Lord. Is it meant to characterize our experience today? Yes. What is its purpose? It is to initiate us deeper into the Spirit's mission and propel us into two areas of the Spirit's work. First, it is meant to draw us deeper into worship and to God. That is the function of other tongues, which we will examine in more detail. Secondly, the Spirit is designed to come upon us to thrust us into the world and the work of the Lord. Worship and work—these are the purposes of the Spirit.

We need the baptism in the Spirit because Jesus himself taught that the work of the Kingdom cannot be done without the baptism in the Spirit. All the things the Lord wants to do in the Church and in the world cannot be done unless we are filled with the Spirit. Many things can be done without His fullness. But the totality of what God wants to do will not be done.

My Pentecostal experience has taught me there is great value in waiting in the Spirit's presence. The

Christian life is not simply intellectual, theological or mind-oriented. It reaches those deeper parts of us that relate to the mystery of the heart in adoration to God. The Spirit reaches into areas of our life where we know what God's will is but are not doing it. And the Spirit forms the character of Christ in us as we allow Him to do so. The Spirit wants to reach into the complacency of our life, where we would be satisfied to live as we are now living. He wants to come upon us and make us earnest about the work of God, make us want God's will and purpose to be done in and through us.

> God would have His Spirit call us out of a life of spiritual complacency to one of deep surrender. Through the Spirit, we can have the joy of hearing from God like we have never heard from Him before.

God would have His Spirit call us out of a life of spiritual complacency to one of deep surrender. Through the Spirit, we can have the joy of hearing from God like we have never heard from Him before. The Spirit is with us at the crossroads of life, as we make the most critical decisions. We need the Spirit of God in an increasingly deeper measure. He wants to open up avenues of worship and of vision to us. May each of us cry out, "Spirit of God, I need You! I can never do this on my own. I can't live the Christian life on my own. I can't know what Your will is on my own. I need You, Holy Spirit."

---

[1] ASV

[2] In 1 Corinthians 12:13, however, that into which we are baptized is the body of Christ: "By one Spirit are we all baptized into one body" (KJV). We can see very clearly that Paul was using the Greek

preposition *en* to mean "by" because wherever he uses the preposition *en* in 1 Corinthians 12, it always indicates a means of something happening. In 1 Corinthians 12:3 we read, "Therefore I tell you that no one who is speaking by the Spirit of God [and it would not be right to translate that "no one speaking in the Spirit of God"] says 'Jesus be cursed.'" In 1 Corinthians 12:9 it says, "To another faith by [not in] the same Spirit, to another gifts of healing by that one Spirit." Paul is saying that by means of the Spirit in conversion we are placed in the body of Christ. And what Jesus is saying in Acts 1:5 is that He is the One who baptizes us in the Spirit.

[3] Luke 4:18, KJV

[4] Acts 2:33

[5] KJV

[6] 1 Chronicles 25:1

[7] NIV

[8] KJV. Some seek to justify their preconception that the baptism in the Spirit and salvation are the same by noting that the aorist participle ("having believed") and the aorist main verb ("did you receive") described coincident rather than sequential events. Such a usage grammatically can be the case as in Matthew 27:4, "I have sinned . . . I have betrayed innocent blood." The sin and the betraying appear as coincident. However, in Matthew 22:25 the aorist participle clearly describes an event which occurred before the action described by the main aorist verb: "having married, he died." Clearly the dying and the marrying are not coincident.

[9] Acts 2:4

[10] Acts 4:31

[11] Acts 6:3

[12] Acts 2:16,17

CHAPTER THREE

ENDURING EVIDENCE

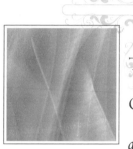

THE WORD *of*

GOD INCREASED;

and the NUMBER

of the DISCIPLES

MULTIPLIED.

—Acts 6:7, KJV

W HEN I WAS TEN YEARS OLD, MY FATHER WAS PASTORING A SMALL CHURCH IN OKLAHOMA. The Latter Rain movement hit with all of the excesses we've seen periodically recycled in the Pentecostal movement. My father was trying to keep the church stable, but there were strong pressures that Dad was not "spiritual" enough. One night, two deacons accosted my dad at the altar. They considered themselves very spiritual. One of the deacons put his fist on my dad's chin and told him to resign. They thought my father was preventing the church from being "spiritual."

Since that time, I've been uncomfortable with the word "spiritual" being used to describe a person or church because it conveys to me an atmosphere in which people have a disconnect between their Spirit-baptized experience and their fruitfulness. As I've handled conflicts among believers over the years, I've found that sometimes the people who use the word "spiritual" in a self-promotional way are really the *least* spiritual.

One of the best tests of a person's spirituality is when you correct them. I compare it to liquid in a glass. When you bump someone holding a glass, whatever is in the glass will spill out. If the glass is filled with water, water will come out. When you "bump" a genuinely Spirit-filled person, you will get love, joy, peace, long-suffering, gentleness, goodness and self-control. But when you bump a person who professes to be Spirit-filled but doesn't have the evidence, out will come

> One of the best tests of a person's spirituality is when you correct them.

meanness, nastiness, bitterness and hostility. In my growing up years, people in church would testify about when they "got it" years ago (referring to the Holy Spirit as an "it"). Some of these people were the nastiest people I knew. Their Spirit baptism that occurred long ago became a medal to wear on their chest, rather than a grace to serve. The enduring work of the Holy Spirit was not evident in their life.

WE MUST NOT STOP

Recently, I was in a conference with two hundred of our national leaders and missionaries from the Middle East, North Africa and Central Asia. In sixteen countries—most of which are very sensitive—the gospel of Jesus Christ is seeing significant advance despite great hardship, threats and persecution.

Over the course of three days, we listened to reports from the delegations in country after country describing the coming of the gospel in power to their lands. I sat with countless numbers of these leaders, including the two young sons of martyrs for the gospel who are now ministers where their fathers laid down their lives.

In many countries and cities where the church did not even exist fifteen years ago, there are now individual congregations numbering more than four thousand people. One such church is only eleven years old but has planted over one hundred other churches. Countries where, two decades ago you could count the number of believers on one hand, now have thousands of believers in Assemblies of God churches.

I ask myself, *How has this happened?* The Lord has impressed me with the fact that these flourishing congregations are demonstrating the "enduring evidence" of the baptism in the Holy Spirit.

In so many of our American churches today, little emphasis is placed on the Holy Spirit. Those of us in leadership, out of concern over this neglect, urge our pastors and churches to pray and provide opportunities for people to receive Spirit baptism with the initial evidence of speaking in other tongues. But, *we must not stop there.*

Pentecostals have always believed and taught that speaking in other tongues is the initial physical evidence. But it is *initial.* We must have the initial evidence, but we must also go past the initial to the *enduring* work of the Spirit. The seventh doctrine of our Statement of Fundamental Truths declares that with the baptism in the Spirit "comes the enduement of power for life and service, the bestowment of the gifts and their uses in the work of the ministry."[1]

> **W**e must have the initial evidence, but we must also go past the initial to the *enduring* work of the Spirit.

This tenet also states: "With the baptism in the Holy Ghost come such experiences as an overflowing fullness of the Spirit,[2] a deepened reverence for God,[3] an intensified consecration to God and dedication to His work,[4] and a more active love for Christ, for His Word, and for the lost."[5]

We believe the baptism in the Spirit brings the delight of initially speaking with other tongues, but if we stop there, this Pentecostal experience will have no ongoing fruitfulness. I grew up in the Assemblies of God when it was preached that the baptism of the Spirit is for the *empowerment* of believers for life and service. In short, the enduring evidence of the baptism in the Spirit results in our fulfilling Acts 1:8. Evangelism and outreach is enduring evidence of the Spirit's work. If we are not seeing this evidence—fruitfulness—we're in trouble.

PRACTICING WHAT WE PREACH

Years ago, Jess Moody wrote a book titled, *A Drink at Joel's Place*. He compared what a church promises to the promises made by a bar. Imagine a bar that promises liquor but the patrons come in and the bartender says, "We're out of liquor today, but we do have milk." The patrons may put up with that for one time, but if it occurs several days in a row, the bar will soon be empty. Similarly, if Kleenex manufacturers began adding a little bit of sandpaper, people would eventually stop using that kind of facial tissue. Or if Coca Cola began adding a dash of lye to their product, you wouldn't continue asking for soft drinks.

As Pentecostals, we also hold out a promise. We say that our churches are graced by the presence of the Holy Spirit. But what if, when people come, there is no sign of His presence, no joy, little love and no manifestation of the grace and power of Christ?

Jess Moody said that we falsely think the label of a thing is what sells it. But, people do not buy Kleenex or Coke because of the brand names. If those companies changed their products, people would stop buying them.

The fact is, we must become what we advertise or we simply have no credibility. A "fighting" Pentecostal church is a contradiction in terms. A Pentecostal church without an emphasis on missions is also a contradiction, as is a

> **T**he fact is, we must become what we advertise or we simply have no credibility.

Pentecostal church without outreach or new believers. In too many of our churches, there is little emphasis placed on people receiving the baptism and fullness of the Spirit. And, we get what we preach or don't preach.

The church is supposed to be what it advertises. Unfortunately, some Pentecostal people have, at one time, had an experience with God, but the work of the Spirit has diminished in their life. It has not continued to affect how they live. I know this firsthand because I receive their critical and judgmental letters. It is amazing to see the disconnect between Spirit baptism and the Spirit-filled life that is found in too many people.

FIVE FACES

Dean Merrill wrote an article called *Five Faces of Pentecost*,[6] in which he talks about the fact that the Pentecostal movement has become huge in the last one hundred years. Assemblies of God fellowships have grown dramatically over the last fifty years, from a million believers to more than sixty million worldwide today. Of the 6.3 billion people on the planet, 2.1 billion call themselves Christians. Of that 2.1 billion, between six and seven hundred million are classified as Pentecostals, charismatics or neocharismatics. In other words, today roughly one-ninth of the population of the world considers themselves Pentecostals.

Merrill categorizes Pentecostals in five ways. The first group, he calls "Retro Pentecost," which refers to a church that is the same as it was decades ago. Merrill compares it to stepping into a kitchen where the appliances are still avocado green. "You walk in and you're slapped in a time warp, vocabulary, music, aesthetics, preaching—all remind you of decades ago. God still uses these people, but they're not as effective in evangelism because the outside world doesn't understand what's going on. It's a wonderful place for the believers who have been there for so long, but things aren't going to change and that's the way it is."

> "Authentic Pentecost" simply means a church which naturally and freely integrates the supernatural into the whole body of biblical truth and practice.

The second group, Merrill calls "Prosperity Pentecost." These are the people you see a lot of on Christian television. He notes that the only rich leader in the New Testament was Barnabas, and he gave away his assets for the Kingdom. This is a keen observation. He notes that "prosperity Pentecost" is the only element of Pentecost that is still regarded by the broader Christian world as cultish.

The third group is "Hyper Pentecost." Hyper Pentecost is sort of like cheerleader Pentecost. If they had a JumboTron, it would be flashing "Get loud! New is good, old is boring." Hyper Pentecost is always looking for the next thing to come down the pike. Merrill says,

"When you're in one of those services, you wonder if you're watching Elijah or the prophets of Baal."

In the fourth group, "Nominal Pentecost," the Pentecostal doctrine is still in the official constitution, but it is lifeless.

The last group is "Authentic Pentecost." This does not mean a church that focuses on tongues and miracles all the time. It simply means a church which naturally and freely integrates the supernatural into the whole body of biblical truth and practice.

AUTHENTIC PENTECOST

Many years ago, an article appeared in a business magazine by a man who had been studying the economic recovery in Brazil after the worst period of inflation. One of the major factors to which he attributed the economic recovery was the Pentecostal revival, especially singling out the Assemblies of God. He interviewed non-Christian factory owners who said they want Assemblies of God employees because they don't come in with a hangover on Monday mornings, they don't steal, and they work a full day. This calls to my remembrance another example.

A man who worked in a factory was known for foul language and telling off-color stories. Friday night after he'd get his paycheck, he would go down to the bar and spend most of his money. By the time he got home, he didn't have much left for groceries or rent that week. One night, he went into a church service and was wonderfully saved and transformed. When he went back to work, he was no longer swearing or telling off-color stories and he was coming home with his full paycheck. His coworkers were not happy with the change in his life. They taunted and ridiculed him. One day, a coworker asked him, "Do you believe Jesus turned water into wine?" He said, "Yes, I do. I wasn't there when it happened. But in my house, He turned beer into furniture." That's a substantive and enduring work of the Spirit.

Many young Pentecostal leaders have reacted to what I call "Pentecostal scholasticism," a view that essentially separates doctrine and practice. It is one thing to academically defend the doctrine of initial evidence—which I do wholeheartedly. But what effect does that have if a disconnect occurs between what we teach and how we behave? We must be sure when speaking of initial evidence that we do far more than defend it with an argument.

The most serious challenge to our doctrine of Spirit baptism comes when there is a lack of evangelism. Statistics show that 52 percent of our churches declined in the last five years. That decline is a direct affront to our doctrine because we believe that Spirit baptism is not only witnessed by initial evidence, but also carries with it empowerment for witness. I am not saying that experience is more important than doctrine, for the opposite is true, and our doctrine would still be true even if every church were declining. However, something is wrong in our experience if the only evidence of Spirit baptism is speaking in tongues. It is the *initial* physical evidence, but *initial* is meant to be followed by a whole train of further evidences.

LEADING BY EXAMPLE

Many people just don't feel the need for the Holy Spirit. This may be because people have seen special gifts misused. I think much of it has to do with people seeing a disconnect between the testimony of those who say they are Spirit-filled and their actual conduct. Jesus talked about how the anxieties and cares of this world can crowd things out. When our life is full of appointments, when we have what we need to make it, when our relationships are going well, we can tend to get comfortable and satisfied, like the Laodicean church—neither hot nor cold. There must be a desire for the Holy Spirit.

I think the reason so many of our young people today are struggling intellectually with the doctrine of initial evidence is because they do not see enough churches with an enduring evidence of the work of the Holy Spirit. The only difference some see between a Pentecostal church and a non-Pentecostal church is that the Pentecostals speak in tongues (and there may not even be much of that!). The younger generation is looking for more than words—they long to witness the demonstration of the Spirit's person, presence and power.

Speaking in tongues as the initial evidence is just the beginning of the baptism in the Holy Spirit; there is far more to the Spirit's fullness! We will have much more credibility in preaching the doctrine of initial evidence if that proclamation is backed up by an ongoing demonstration of the Spirit's power. His power propels believers into this world with an anointing to witness, a lifestyle like that of Jesus—a boldness to heal the sick in body and heart, to cast out demons, and to bring good news to the poor.

This is an hour for us as Pentecostals to proclaim with new fervor both the baptism and fullness of the Holy Spirit. Speaking in tongues is that initial dynamic that catapults our experience beyond the natural into the supernatural. But if that's all there is, we will be like a rocket launched into space that, instead of going into orbit, plunges to the ground. The baptism in the Holy Spirit is God's great rocket booster to lift us past what the flesh can do and into the orbit of supernatural usefulness to fulfill the Great Commission of our Lord. The orbit God wants for us is that "the word of God spread . . . The number of disciples . . . increased."[7]

It is vital that pastors and ministers live a life full of the Spirit and call people to experience Spirit baptism and receive the fullness of the Holy Spirit. Early Pentecostals did not try to argue people into the baptism in the Spirit. They lived and preached in such a way that people wanted what they had. If we have nothing to give but arguments and theological defenses of our doctrinal position, this generation will seek spiritual reality elsewhere. I am not saying that apologetics are unimportant. Clearly, we must be able to give a reason for the doctrines we hold. But we must acknowledge that there will be no lack of people responding to the work of the Spirit when they see a demonstration of the reality of the Spirit's presence and power.

I want to exhort all of us to stir up the fire and preach not only the initial evidence, but the enduring evidence of Spirit baptism. If we only have the initial evidence but no empowerment, our young people will no longer be interested in the initial evidence. But, if they see the enduring evidence—the empowerment which brings people to Christ and grows the church while God performs signs and wonders among us—then they will want the initial evidence of Spirit baptism as the gateway to the substantive and ongoing evidence of living a Spirit-filled life.

———————

[1] Luke 24:49; Acts 1:4,8; 1 Corinthians 12:1-31

[2] John 7:37–39; Acts 4:8

[3] Acts 2:43; Hebrews 12:28

[4] Acts 2:42

[5] Mark 16:20

[6] Merrill, Dean. *Five Faces of Pentecost* was a presentation given at the Christian Life College Fall Festival, Mount Prospect, Illinois, on November 15, 2005.

[7] Acts 6:7

CHAPTER FOUR

THE SPIRIT AND SPEAKING IN TONGUES

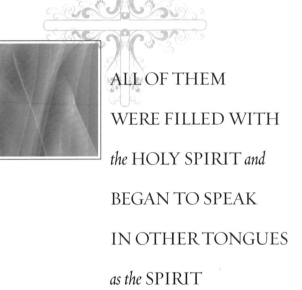

ALL OF THEM
WERE FILLED WITH
the HOLY SPIRIT *and*
BEGAN TO SPEAK
IN OTHER TONGUES
as the SPIRIT
ENABLED THEM.

—Acts 2:4

N ADDITION TO GLORIFYING JESUS CHRIST IN OUR LIFE AND REACHING THE WORLD for the Lord, the Spirit touches the depths of our being. If we understand our nature as spirit, soul and body, as Paul revealed in 1 Thessalonians 5:23, our outward being is the body. Then, there is an inner component to us. The Greek word is *psyche*, from which we get our English word *psyche* which translates as soul. But there is an even deeper component: the *pneuma*, the spirit—our nuclear core. God seeks to reach us there.

The soul and spirit are the aspect Jesus spoke of in John 7, on the last day of the Feast, "If any man is thirsty, let him come to Me and drink. He who believes in Me, as the Scripture said, 'From his *innermost being* shall flow rivers of living water.'"[1]

Jesus said that when the Holy Spirit comes upon us, He reaches all dimensions of our being. He comes into the essential core of where we live, from where everything about us proceeds. As the Spirit comes and we drink of Him, then out of our innermost being— that centering of our personality—comes rivers of living water.

RIVER OF THE SPIRIT

"Streams" of living water is often used in John 7, but I've discovered the Greek word translated here— *potamos*—always represents a considerable body of water. The word *rivers* more clearly describes it.

The same word in Matthew 7:27 is translated

floods, when "the floods came, . . . and beat upon that house"[2] that was built by the foolish builder. In 2 Corinthians 11:26, Paul uses the same word to talk about being "in perils of waters"[3] when he was in trouble on the seas. Revelation 22:1 uses the word in reference to a great river of life. Also, the Jordan River and the great Euphrates River, both considerable bodies of water in biblical days, are described by this same word.

Jesus said that when we have drunk of the Spirit, then out of our inner being will flow not a small trickle of water, not even a stream, but a surging, powerful river of water. Somehow the Spirit of God takes our personality and does something marvelous—allowing the personality and the power and the character of Jesus to flow from us. John explained this statement of Jesus: "By this he meant the Spirit, whom those who believed in him were later to receive. Up to that time the Spirit had not been given, since Jesus had not yet been glorified."[4]

Speaking in tongues is part of this flowing of the Spirit of God, reaching upward in worship, outward in concern for the world, and inward to build up the inner man.

When does this flowing out take place? John said that experience did not begin until Jesus was glorified (risen and ascended into heaven). The Spirit was not yet considered as "given" even though in John 20:22 the disciples had received the conversion work of the Lord when He breathed on them. They received the Spirit, but that is not counted as the Spirit being "given" in the way to which Jesus referred at the Feast.

Jesus was referring to the Day of Pentecost when 120 of the disciples for the first time drink of the Spirit who is outpoured. Out of their inner being flowed a river of the Spirit which reached out in three directions—a river of praise flowing upward to God in worship, a river flowing outward in evangelism, and a river flowing inward in edification. When you look at the work of the Spirit in your life, He's always working in all those directions—up, out and in.

Speaking in tongues is part of this flowing of the Spirit of God, reaching upward in worship, outward in concern for the world, and inward to build up the inner man. Tongues is not the entirety of the river. Neither can it be isolated from the river of the Spirit.

WHY DID GOD CHOOSE TONGUES?

The Day of Pentecost was a time of incredible joy. It's not surprising when we read that the disciples were so overcome with joy while speaking in other tongues that the observers thought they were drunk.

The wind and the fire never reappear, but speaking in tongues continues. Examples include Cornelius's household at Ephesus and Paul's letter to the Corinthians, in which he addressed the use of tongues both in public meetings and in private prayer.

Why did God choose tongues? This side of heaven, we may never fully know. But, even if we do not fully know the *why*, we do know the *what*. God did choose tongues.

The tongue often represents the impurity that pours out of our hearts. James dealt with the sins of the tongue.[5] He compared the tongue to a rudder that guides a large boat, or a small spark that sets a forest on fire. "The tongue also is a fire, a world of evil among the parts of the body. It corrupts the whole person, sets the whole course of his life on fire, and is itself set on fire by hell."[6]

The tongue can express sinful anger. What do we do when we lose our temper? Our tongue spews out what is in the heart. Paul told us to forsake wrath, anger and clamor.[7] The tongue lies, speaks profanity, releases criticism, and grumbles. The tongue emits foul and foolish talk: "Nor should there be obscenity, foolish talk or coarse joking, which are out of place, but rather thanksgiving."[8]

God fixes these problems and enables the tongue to be a source of good and blessing.

1. The tongue gives definition to what we experience.

Jesus told us about the power of words that can move mountains.[9]

What were the tongues expressing on the Day of Pentecost? Luke recorded, "We hear them declaring the wonders of God in our own tongues."[10]

The word translated *wonders* is *megaleios*, which means "magnificent, grand, great, sublime or beautiful." Speaking in other tongues allows us to express the absolute glory of God. It declares the reality of the Spirit being poured out on us.

2. The tongue gives us the ability to communicate readily.

Without speaking, try to tell someone the happiest moment in your life. Or, if you have been somewhere awesome and beautiful, try to describe it verbally. You really cannot fit it all into words—it is an experience. Speaking in other tongues helps us express the magnitude of something that goes beyond our ability to use the verbs, nouns and adjectives we know. We are enabled to talk to God about His wonders.

3. The tongue expresses what is in the heart.

In John 21, the Lord asked Peter three times, "Do you love me?" Peter's response shows us what was in his heart.

There are two forms of human communication: verbal and nonverbal. For example, an embrace is nonverbal. You love so much that words just don't adequately express how you feel.

How do we tell God that we love Him? With words? Yes. With deeds? Yes. But God has also provided another way, a very intimate way—speaking in other tongues. We cannot physically reach out and put our arms around the Lord, so the Holy Spirit has given us this unique gift that helps us express intimacy with Him.

Romans 8:26 says, "The Spirit himself intercedes for us with groans that words cannot express." In other words, longings, heartaches and aspirations that cannot be imprisoned within the confines of our own vocabularies, well up from the spiritual and psychological depths in us. This is the kind of thing that Hannah experienced in her prayer to God, "I was pouring out my soul to the Lord."[11] Psalm 62:8 says, "Trust in him at all times, O people; pour out your hearts to him, for God is our refuge."

4. Tongues is part of the promise of the Father.

Acts 1:4,5: "On one occasion, while he was eating with them, he gave them this command: 'Do not leave Jerusalem, but wait for the gift my Father promised, which you have heard me speak about. For John baptized with water, but in a few days you will be baptized with the Holy Spirit.'"

Acts 2:4: "All of them were filled with the Holy Spirit and began to speak in others tongues as the Spirit enabled them."

Acts 2:33: "Exalted to the right hand of God, he has received from the Father the promised Holy Spirit, and has poured out what you now see and hear."

Acts 2:39: "The promise is for you and your children and for all who are far off—for all whom the Lord our God will call."

Speaking in tongues was an integral part of that wonderful occasion.

Although there are mysteries concerning tongues, this does not mean that tongues are without meaning. Even though we do not understand that meaning, the Spirit is praying through us.

In addition to "unknown tongues," there are many instances in which the Spirit enables believers to speak in a language that they have never learned. While no one present may recognize the language, on occasion, someone may understand what is said. There are many examples of this occurrence.

Many years ago, Gospel Publishing House published a book by Ralph Harris called, *Spoken by the Spirit*, in which many accounts of this were reported.

DEFINITIONS OF TONGUES

A common term used for speaking in tongues is *glossolalia*. Three basic definitions have been given to *glossa*, or tongue. Two of them are biblical and one of them is in error.

The first definition of *tongue* refers to the organ of speech. In the New Testament, for example, when the poor man Lazarus was in Abraham's bosom, the rich man in hell wanted Lazarus to dip his finger in water and cool the rich man's tongue. The word for tongue there is the same word used in Acts 2:4, "speak in other tongues."

A second definition that has been put to *glossa* is "ecstatic utterance." This is how "tongues" has been translated in some versions of the Bible, such as *The New English Bible*, Barclay's Bible, Williams Bible and the *Goodspeed* Bible. In 1 Corinthians 12:10, which describes the gift of tongues, the term used by these translators is "ecstatic utterance."

However, *ecstasy* is not an appropriate word scripturally to use of a person who is speaking in tongues. I want to be very exact on the meaning of the word *ecstasy*. It is from two Greek words that mean "out of" and "being." Therefore, ecstasy is the condition of a person who is *out of being*. A person who is ecstatic has momentarily gotten leave of himself and is in a trance. The word is used seven times in the New Testament. Three times it is used of Peter and Paul, not as they spoke in tongues but in reference to great visions. Four other times, it is used to describe people's reactions to miracles. Ecstasy is never used in Scripture to describe a person speaking in tongues.

Some people think that in order to speak in tongues you must get into a subconscious or semiconscious state. Then, when you have let yourself drift into this state, the Spirit takes over and does everything. Nothing could be further from a scriptural definition. The person who ministers in the spiritual gift of tongues or in prophecy is in control. The Spirit is enabling the person's speech, but the believer also is functioning with rationality.

> **T**he person who ministers in the spiritual gift of tongues or in prophecy is in control. The Spirit is enabling the person's speech, but the believer also is functioning with rationality.

The third way *glossa* is used means simply to speak a language. There are various descriptions of this in the New Testament. Jesus promised the disciples "they will speak with new tongues."[12] In Acts 2:4, it says they "began to speak in other tongues." Acts 2 is the only example in the New Testament where speaking in other tongues refers to clearly discernable human languages. They were languages not learned by the speaker but they were recognizable by the audience.

Then there are diverse tongues.[13] These represent different kinds of tongues. Sometimes, as we speak in tongues, we find ourselves speaking in a different way than a past work of the Spirit in us.

Fourth, there is what the King James Version calls "unknown tongues." Although the word *unknown* is not in the Greek text, it is used five times in the King James Version.[14] The King James Version uses *unknown* because *tongues* in those verses always contrasts with traditional speech or intelligible speech.

TONGUES AND THE BAPTISM IN THE SPIRIT

It is important to look at the whole dimension of how tongues is referenced in the New Testament. There are four ways that tongues function in the believer and in the church. The first way that tongues, or glossolalia, function is in relationship to the baptism in the Spirit.

There are several examples of tongues as a sign of the baptism in the Spirit. The first instance is in Acts 2:4: "And they were all filled with the Holy Spirit and began to speak with other tongues, as the Spirit was giving them utterance."[15] On the Day of Pentecost, we find that when all were baptized in the Spirit, all spoke in tongues. The Scriptures do not say that some prophesied, some did works of healing, some exercised discernment, some gave utterances in tongues, and some interpreted tongues. In Acts 2:4, glossolalia is part of the experience of all who received the Spirit.

The second reference to Spirit baptism is in Acts 8:14–17. When the apostles in Jerusalem heard that Samaria had received the word of God, they sent Peter and John. The Samaritans had already believed in Jesus and had been baptized in water, but they had not yet received the Spirit. Peter and John laid hands upon them that they might receive the Spirit. However, there is no reference to tongues on that occasion as on the Day of Pentecost, so some are quick to assume Pentecost must have been a unique experience. But I think that is too simplistic a view of the text.

There are clues within the text that something happened when the Spirit came upon the Samaritans. In verse 18, Simon the Sorcerer saw outward evidence that the Spirit was given, and he offered the apostles money to be able to do the same thing. In verse 16, the Greek literally says the Spirit had not yet "fallen upon" the Samaritans. We can connect the Samaritans' experience in Acts 8 with Acts 10:44. At Cornelius's house, while Peter was speaking, the Holy Spirit "fell" upon all those who were hearing the Word and they began to speak with other tongues. In Acts 11:15, Peter said the Spirit "fell" upon Cornelius "as He did upon us at the beginning."[16]

Acts 9:17 is a third instance of the baptism in the Spirit. After Saul was converted on the road to Damascus, the Lord sent Ananias to lay hands on him that he might receive the Spirit and his sight. Here again, we are not told Paul spoke in tongues on that occasion. But by using the process of induction we come to the conclusion in 1 Corinthians 14 that tongues were a regular part of Paul's prayer life.

A fourth instance occurs in Acts chapters 10 and 11, when the Spirit came upon Cornelius and his family and they received the Spirit. The Spirit fell upon them and they spoke with other tongues. When Peter reported back to the Jerusalem church, he said, "The Holy Spirit came on them as he had come on us at the beginning."[17] Why would we want to settle for anything less than what they had at the beginning?

Finally, the fifth instance takes places in Ephesus in Acts 19:1–7. Once more, believers received the Spirit and spoke in tongues. In AD 55, about twenty-five years after Paul's conversion experience, he came to a group of about twelve followers of John the Baptist at Ephesus. The first question he asked them was, "Have ye received the Holy Ghost since ye believed?"[18] Then he laid hands upon them and they received the Spirit and spoke in other tongues.

Of the five instances in Acts when people clearly receive the Spirit, three instances explicitly mention that people spoke in tongues. In Paul's experience, it is clear he regularly spoke in tongues and it is logical to assume his beginning experience would be identical to that of the Day of Pentecost. And at Samaria, likewise, the Spirit fell upon believers in a manner reminiscent of Pentecost.

TONGUES AND SPIRITUAL GIFTS

We would expect from this understanding of Scripture that tongues is an aspect and component of Spirit baptism. This is, however, not the only purpose of tongues in the New Testament. Tongues is also one of the nine gifts of the Spirit.

In 1 Corinthians 12:30, Paul asked in reference to these gifts, "Do all speak in tongues?" The obvious answer is no, not all speak in tongues. There are some who say, "There's your answer right there. Tongues is not always a part of an experience with the baptism in the Spirit." But in this case, Paul is describing a gathering of believers when someone stands and gives an utterance and someone else interprets it. The difference between tongues on that occasion and tongues in the personal use is that Paul is dealing in that passage with the gifts of the Spirit that relate to the common good.

But, Paul turned right around and said, "I would like every one of you to speak in tongues, but I would rather have you prophesy."[19] In essence, Paul is saying, "On the personal level, I'd like every one of you to speak in tongues. But in the church, prophesy." In a public setting, prophesying or preaching or testifying to the Word of God is far more appropriate than many people giving utterances in tongues.

Paul said in 1 Corinthians 14:18,19: "I thank God that I speak in tongues more than all of you. But in the church I would rather speak five intelligible words to instruct others than ten thousand words in a tongue." Therefore, when there is an utterance of tongues in the church, it is not God sending a message to us as much as it is an utterance of prayer, praise, petition or intercession going up to God. Tongues is associated with a special gift when we are gathered together as the body of Christ.

THE SPIRIT AND SPEAKING IN TONGUES • 97

When I was freshman at Evangel College in 1958, we had a revival that fall. During one of the evening chapel services, someone gave an utterance in tongues and it was followed by an interpretation. The interpretation was given by a young woman who, to my knowledge, had never exercised any spiritual gifts before. In our dorm later that night, Arthur Cao, a student from Taiwan, was overcome with emotion. He said, "I've been very discouraged. I'm away from home and family, in a foreign land and I just wondered if God knew where I was. The utterance in tongues tonight was in Mandarin, my native language. And the interpretation was a perfect translation. It was such an encouragement and comfort to me—that God knew where I was." It was a remarkable impression on me as a college freshman to be a part of an experience like that.

TONGUES AND THE BELIEVER

Third, tongues is a personal language of prayer. First Corinthians 14:2 says, "Anyone who speaks in a tongue does not speak to men but to God." Prayer addresses God. Prayer is composed of praise, thanksgiving, petition, confession and intercession. When I speak to God in an unknown tongue, I often find myself thanking God and am very aware that I am praising Him in a way my rational mind cannot comprehend. I find myself interceding for people, countries, regions and large-scale needs in a way I do not understand.

I think we can find ourselves also confessing deep dimensions of our personality that even our rationality does not understand. There's much about our personality we do not know. Hidden marks have been left upon our life from the past. We need to be healed from devastating emotional scars that we may have blocked out of our consciousness. Tongues can be a part of that healing.

Paul said in Romans 8:26,27 that there are difficult times when we don't know how to pray as we should. But the Spirit intercedes for us with groanings that cannot be uttered, that are too deep for words.

Tongues is not defined in Scripture as the language of evangelism. Some have looked at the Day of Pentecost and said, "The early disciples didn't have enough time to learn all the languages of the world, so God gave them new languages so they could preach about Him immediately." Many early Pentecostals erroneously believed they wouldn't

> Tongues is also a means by which our noncognitive side can reach out to God.

have to learn the language of a country where they were called. They quickly learned when they arrived that they were mistaken.

But when the 120 were done speaking in tongues in Acts 2, the nonbelievers were confused, amazed and some of them even mocked the believers. Tongues attracted their attention, but what quickened their hearts and brought results for the gospel was Peter's message in the Aramaic language, which everyone understood.

Though it is a rare occurrence, there have been accounts of AG missionaries who have spoken in the Spirit languages they had never learned in an evangelistic context. There have been accounts of nonbelievers in a church service who have heard an understandable language from someone who was speaking in tongues and the Spirit convicted the nonbelievers. But these are signs of the Spirit's presence, not the language of evangelism. The language of prayer may reach out and confront someone with a powerful sign of God's presence. Tongues is speech toward God, a personal language of prayer.

Tongues will edify, or build up, the believer.[20] This is a ministry of the Holy Spirit. I find it impossible in my own spiritual life to pray in tongues when I am angry or I have sinned. I only find it possible to really, purely pray in tongues when things are right between me and the Lord and between me and others. I find it is then that praying in tongues really builds up.

Tongues is also a means by which our noncognitive side can reach out to God. This is why Paul said, "I will pray with the spirit, and I will pray with the understanding also: I will sing with the spirit, and I will sing with the understanding also."[21] Here, he was speaking of praying and singing in tongues as compared to praying and singing in a language he knew. In our relationship with God, the noncognitive side of us needs to be "caught up" in God as well.

TONGUES AND THE NONBELIEVER

The fourth thing tongues represents in the New Testament is a sign to nonbelievers.[22] This is an extremely difficult passage to interpret. On the one hand, Paul said tongues is a sign to nonbelievers. Then he turned around and said if nonbelievers are present, don't speak in tongues unless they are interpreted. So we're left with a kind of conundrum.

Some think Paul was using irony here. Evidently, the Corinthians were judging the spirituality or success of a service by the presence of tongues, and Paul would have refuted that practice. He may have been saying, "If you need tongues as a sign of God's presence, then you're an unbeliever." Paul was perfectly capable of using irony.

But Paul was talking about the dimension of tongues in which clear languages are understood by a listener, such as the Day of Pentecost, when it is a sign. While people came to salvation on the Day of Pentecost because of the preached Word, tongues were a sign of God's presence. Therefore, when a nonbeliever comes in who understands a tongue that is spoken, it will indeed be a sign to that person.

I believe anytime believers come together and people speak in other tongues both precognitive speech, which we talked about earlier, and languages someone present might recognize can occur. We don't know whether we're praying in an earthly language that has grammar, syntax and vocabulary, or if we're praying in a precognitive speech that is just the pouring out of our heart to God. Each has the capacity to alert the heart of the nonbeliever to God's presence.

TONGUES AND THE GREAT COMMISSION

The baptism in the Spirit relates not only to our worship but also to our mission as Christians. The infilling of the Spirit is an empowering experience. People often take the word *power* from the Greek word *dunamis*, from which we derive the English word *dynamite*. So, some think this relates to explosive power. But I've discovered that the more adequate definition of *dunamis* is *capability*.

As followers of Christ, we too often live as shy people with inferiority complexes, people who find it difficult to work up the courage to witness to someone. We need the Spirit of God to fill us. The Spirit gives us the authority and the capability to do whatever God has called us to do. We cannot do things for God if there's not a peace and joy in our heart. The Spirit builds up the inner man, preparing us to go out with the gospel.

> **T**he Spirit gives us the authority and the capability to do whatever God has called us to do.

Jesus told His disciples to wait in Jerusalem until they had been endued with power from on high. I believe the 120 in the Upper Room were there not simply to receive a personal spiritual experience. I believe they were there because they had embraced what Jesus had said. They may not have fully understood it, but they were offering themselves as a corporate body to do the Lord's work in whatever way the Lord would appoint them. They had already begun to identify and accept the mission He had given them—to be His witnesses in Jerusalem, Judea, Samaria and to the ends of the earth. As they were in the process of embracing that mission, the Spirit came upon them and filled them with praise, and then out of that praise came the power to be His witnesses.

A pastor once told me that when he was child in 1955, his dad was the Sunday School superintendent in Luxor, Arkansas. His father took him to the storefront church, along with a guest who was to speak that evening—a missionary who had returned from China six years earlier. It was custom for there to be prayer before the service, with the men going into one room and the women another. As they entered, an old grandma in the women's prayer room was praying in the Spirit. The missionary listened awhile and then said, "That lady is praying for the members of my church in China, and calling out every name." The missionary was my dad.

. . . Spirit baptism is not something we ask for once. It should be something we ask for, and expect to receive, repeatedly.

Pastor Campbell told me that this experience left an indelible mark on him. He now pastors a church founded by his father, in a town that has about fifty people, who are very poor.

He had an average attendance of about thirty, when the Lord impressed on him that they should do more to support missions and build a bigger church. Over the next five years, that little church gave fifty thousand dollars to missions.

But even more than that, the members got enthused about giving to missions and decided to *become* missionaries themselves. They started inviting their neighbors and coworkers to church, along with local drug addicts and even drug dealers! To everyone's amazement, people began to accept the invitations, and lives began to change.

Today, the church has an average of 120 in attendance each Sunday, and the church facilities are paid in full. They support twenty-six missionaries, and in the last five years have given over two hundred thousand dollars to missions.

Each of us should pray, "God, send me into this community for You!" Some may say, "Lord, how do I do it? I'm not an evangelist. I don't know how to knock on doors and witness to someone." The Holy Spirit is saying to us, "I will come upon you with power. I'll open the door. Just offer yourself to Me. Be candidates for My power. Expect Me to move!" The Holy Spirit will come.

LIVING IN CONTINUAL SPIRIT BAPTISM

When praying for the baptism in the Spirit as a young person, I would hear people use Luke 11:9–13 to teach about seeking the Baptism—ask, seek, knock. But I misunderstood these verses. I really didn't think the Holy Spirit wanted to have anything to do with me. I felt that I not only had to ask, but I had to beat the door down.

In reality, this passage reminds us that Spirit baptism is not something we ask for once. It should be something we ask for, and expect to receive, repeatedly. This is why Jesus used the progressive present tense. Go on asking, go on seeking, go on knocking. There is never any time in our life where we simply come to rest and say, "I've received all the Spirit of God I'll ever need."

We never have enough of God's Spirit. Yes, we have enough to serve God capably today, but we must replenish the supply of His presence in succeeding days. Jesus gave us a pattern to follow—ask, seek and knock. If you're not filled to the level of your need for the Spirit today, then ask, seek and knock. And go on asking, seeking and knocking, until you're full and satisfied for that moment. Then, there will come another moment where you'll need more of the Spirit. It's right to say, "Father, You promised the Spirit. You promised the baptism in the Spirit. I'm here to ask."

In doing this, we need to examine our hearts. The Holy Spirit desires to fill a clean vessel. He is the *Holy* Spirit. Psalm 139:23,24 says, "Search me, O God, and know my heart; test me and know my anxious thoughts. See if there is any offensive way in me, and lead me in the way everlasting." There is value to laying our life before God and saying, "Lord, I want Your Holy Spirit in a deep way, but there is unconfessed sin in my life." The Holy Spirit wants our life to be clean. Examine your heart.

> **W**e never have enough of God's Spirit. Yes, we have enough to serve God capably today, but we must replenish the supply of His presence in succeeding days.

We must also release ourself to the Spirit's ministry. Jesus has promised to fill us with the Spirit. The Spirit seeks to well up within us. That's why speaking in tongues is so much akin to an artesian well. The question is often asked, "Can you receive the baptism in the Spirit without speaking in tongues?" I ask, "Can you be baptized in water without getting wet?" A baptism involves more than water, but it's impossible to be baptized without getting wet. There's a sense in which speaking in another language is the inward release that the Spirit wants in our life.

Don't treat the baptism in the Spirit as something that happens only once. Exercise the gift. Paul said to Timothy about his ministry in 2 Timothy 1:6, "stir up the gift of God, which is in thee by the putting on of my hands."[23] The New International Version says, "fan into flame." The word for "stir up" is a Greek word that represents a hot coal, an ember, a spark. A charcoal fire needs to be fanned into flame. This is the word Paul used. We need times when the wind of the Spirit of God rekindles a gift for ministry. This is true with the baptism in the Spirit as well. Kindle, rekindle, keep being filled with the Spirit so that this blessed experience is a regular expression of your relationship with Christ.

---

[1] John 7:37,38, NASB, italics added

[2] KJV

[3] KJV

[4] John 7:39

[5] 3:2–6

[6] 3:6

[7] Ephesians 4:31, Colossians 3:8

[8] Ephesians 5:4

[9] Matthew 17:20

[10] Acts 2:11

[11] 1 Samuel 1:15

[12] Mark 16:17, NASB

[13] 1 Corinthians 12:10, KJV

[14] 1 Corinthians 14:2,4,14,19,27

[15] NASB

[16] NASB

[17] Acts 11:15

[18] Acts 19:2, KJV

[19] 1 Corinthians 14:5

[20] 1 Corinthians 14:4

[21] 1 Corinthians 14:15, KJV

[22] 1 Corinthians 14:20–22

[23] KJV

CHAPTER FIVE

THE FRUIT OF
THE SPIRIT

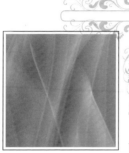

BUT *the* FRUIT *of the* SPIRIT IS LOVE, JOY, PEACE, PATIENCE, KINDNESS, GOODNESS, FAITHFULNESS, GENTLENESS *and* SELF-CONTROL.

—Galatians 5:22,23

I T'S ONE THING TO RECEIVE CHRIST IN OUR LIFE AND ACKNOWLEDGE HIM AS OUR SAVIOR AND LORD. But there is a process in which He actually becomes Lord and is formed in us so that the personality of Jesus moves into our personality. We express through our own uniqueness the common characteristics and personality that really belong to Jesus. I've found that the more I become like Jesus the more uniquely I become myself. We don't all look like we're made from the same mold in terms of our personality. We're all still different. But there is a thread that unites us together because Christ is formed in us. When Christ is formed in us, it means His personality will be duplicated in us.

When we look at Galatians 5:22,23, we read what the fruit of the Spirit is. But this could also describe what Jesus is. We could say that because Jesus is loving, we are loving. Because He is joyful, we are joyful. Because He is peaceful, we are peaceful. And right on down through the list. There is a commonality that links the fruit of the Spirit to the personality of Jesus and to our own personality.

As you look at the New Testament carefully, you will see that bearing fruit often is in direct proportion to our difficulties. These difficulties are not easy to bear. The Galatian letter was written to people who came out of what we now know as south central Turkey. It was a very difficult area in which to launch the gospel. In every city described in Acts 13 and 14, there were tumultuous times for the apostle Paul—times when he was kicked out of

town after town and in one place pelted with rocks until
he almost died. That's not a tranquil environment.

If you think having the fruit of the Spirit in your
life is only possible when you have a lot of time on your
hands, an ability to spend hours sitting under a tree
reading, then you don't understand the fruit. If we all
had this ideal environment, we could develop a
semblance of the fruit of the Spirit. But the great thing
about the fruit of the Spirit is that it operates in difficulties. It's really seen most clearly then. In writing to the
Galatians, Paul knew they had seen the fruit of the Spirit
in his life when he had been under extreme pressure and
adversity. God's Spirit in us works whether the tempera-
ture is emotionally cold or hot. In all kinds of temperatures, the Spirit of God is seeking to bear fruit.

The fruit of the Spirit can't be confused with the
gifts of the Spirit. The twenty-four gifts in the New
Testament are plural. They apply to our life in correspondence with our natural inclinations on many occasions
and with the needs of the body of Christ. None of us have
all the gifts. Only Christ operates with all the gifts.

But that's not the case with the fruit of the Spirit.
We do not hunt and pick through the fruit of the Spirit
saying, "I'll take this one, but I'd rather leave that one
behind." In fact, when some people talk about the fruit of
the Spirit, they mistakenly refer to it as the *fruits* of the
Spirit. But the language of the Scripture, both in the original and in the English, is very clear. It is the *fruit* of the
Spirit, not fruits. Therefore, all these characteristics listed
in Galatians 5:22,23 are meant to be part of our life.

LOVE

The first fruit of the Spirit is love. Some have said this really is the fruit out of which all the other fruit comes. There really are not nine fruits of the Spirit. There really is only one—love. If you have love, you have everything else.

All the fruit of the Spirit has a parallel in non-Christian experience. There are non-Christians who are very loving people. What makes Christian love different is that it does not flow out of emotion and feeling. It flows out of commitment. Christian love is known by its extent, by the degree to which it will go. Human love is so often based upon attraction. We love those who are somehow attractive to us. But everyone's idea of beauty is different. It's easy to love people who look good.

It's also easy to love if the love is returned. Romantic love depends on reciprocity. Paul said in Romans 5 that God loved us while we were yet sinners. When we were unattractive and when there was no love being returned to Him, Jesus still loved us. He loved to the length and to the limit that He went to the cross for us to show the extent of His love. Christian love not only loves those within the family but also goes beyond the family to love those who are in extreme need. This is the fruit the Lord seeks to develop in our life, an enduring love generated out of our commitment to Christ.

The New Testament never takes for granted that we know how to love. In Romans 12:9–21, a list of prescriptions is given to help us love one another—from entertaining strangers and showing hospitality to honoring one another and returning good for evil. The New Testament is very clear in outlining how we ought to love. So Christ reaches into us through our prayers, attitudes and actions to shape us and help us become loving people.

You may not be where you would like to be in your capacity to love. But the fruit is developmental. It will take you where you are now and grow from there. One of the most important things about love is to quit looking for someone to love you. We all might say, "I'd be a better person if someone loved me more." That may well be true, but we don't have power or control over what someone else does. Christ has not given us a spirit of fear but of power, love and self-control. The Lord says, "Don't spend your time *looking* for love. Rather, spend your time seeking to give love. Find ways of expressing love through words, actions and attitudes."

JOY

The second fruit of the Spirit is joy. There are varieties of joy we share with non-Christians. The celebrative moments in our life—weddings, births, engagements— are great sources of joy. Achievements—breaking the sales record in the office or graduating with honors— bring joy when we have worked hard and reached a goal. Relationships bring joy when we feel things are right between us and another person.

Life often brings joy even for the nonbeliever, but it is different from the fruit of the Spirit. Some non-Christians seem very happy, but we know from our own experience in coming to Christ, and from the Bible itself, that even the happiest non-Christian endures a void, an emptiness, an aching only Christ can fill.

Uniquely, Christian joy—the fruit of joy—begins with our salvation. In talking about salvation in Luke 15, Jesus told the stories of the lost sheep, the lost coin and the lost son. Why? Because these figures of speech spoke of salvation. Our Heavenly Father rejoices over us when we are saved. It's a time for joy.

One of the dimensions of joy in the New Testament is the joy of the gospel coming to others. When we see someone else saved and come to the Lord, we rejoice. This is a dimension of joy that we don't focus upon enough. In John 4:36, Jesus talked about the ones who go out sowing and reaping and rejoice together. In Acts 15:3, when the Early Church heard of the conversion of the Gentiles, they rejoiced over what God had done.

There is joy associated with the infilling of the Spirit in Acts 2:13. The joy is so deep that the 120 were mistakenly assumed to be drunk. But the Spirit does bring joy. Thank God there are those great celebration moments in worship when our hearts truly sing and we are literally outside of ourselves.

Christian joy is even present in the midst of struggle and stress and suffering. "We also rejoice in our sufferings."[1] Who rejoices in suffering? Christian joy finds us even in our down times and we rejoice because we know that even in our suffering, God is working out a process in our life. This process is initiated with suffering but goes on to develop endurance—another fruit of the Spirit—and character, that which we are when all the masks are removed.

We rejoice also in our future hope. Jesus said in Matthew 5:12, "Rejoice and be glad, because great is your reward in heaven." We have not yet even begun to consider the glories of heaven. Many times we're even reticent to speak about heaven and the afterlife because of the criticism that we are "pie-in-the-sky" people. But we should have joy, uniquely Christian joy, in our future hope. A great day is coming.

The Scriptures give us many ways to keep the joy flowing. We nurture joy as we love, sing and give thanks. Singing and nurturing an attitude of thanksgiving are necessary corollaries to joy.

PEACE

The third fruit of the Spirit is peace. This arises out of God's grace. When love and joy, the fruit of the Spirit, are present, they naturally produce a person who is at peace. When the Scripture talks about peace, it is not simply describing cessation of conflict. Life is filled with conflict.

In the Scriptures, the great Hebrew word *shalom* (translated "peace") means wholeness, well-being, fulfilling one's purpose for life. A peaceful person is living out his or her dreams—not living in a fantasy world, but living with a sense of wholeness, balance and well-being. We need that kind of gyrocompass in our life—that in the center of us is peace. We must be comfortable with who we are, no longer trying to be like someone else or match up to their expectation of us. How many of us are driven in life by what other people think? Some of us are even driven by expectations of people who are now dead. In our hearts there is no fixed center of rest.

A person of peace is resolving hostility in his or her life, especially towards those who are against them. They're using what Jesus taught us to do with the people who take our peace from us—pray for them, bless them, speak well of them, do good to them. A person of peace is forgiving and resolves anger daily. "Do not let the sun go down while you are still angry."[2] You can be at peace as you do these things.

A person at peace depends on God to resolve stress. There may be many responsibilities and pressures, but God is in control and He can help us to live with the strength we need for today. We can sit still in God's presence and be the person He made us to be. We are content with that. We are at peace.

PATIENCE

The fourth fruit of the Spirit is patience. God's patience cannot be developed without adversity. Patience comes about by situations in our life that would make us impatient. There are two Greek words translated in the New Testament as *patience*. The word used in Galatians 5:22 means movement of air or water, and gradually came to be used to describe anger—a movement, a violent movement, to well up, to boil up, to blow up. So, patience is "long anger"—a person who takes a long time to boil up, well up and blow up, not a quick-fused person.

Another Greek word is used interchangeably in the New Testament on several occasions. It describes a person who "remains under." When we're praying for God to do something in our life, we may be carrying a load. He can either give us strength to carry the load or He can remove the load from our back. This translation of *patience* means strength to carry the load—to remain under.

The only way you get the chance to develop patience is by finding those impatient circumstances of life. Patience is an attribute of God, for it describes His willingness to be long-suffering on our behalf. When you're loving and joyful and peaceful, somehow patience easily slides into that growing development of the fruit of the Spirit.

KINDNESS

Kindness, the fifth fruit of the Spirit, comes from a Greek word akin to *Christ* or *Messiah*. I think those words in the Greek beautifully match one another. Of the seventeen times the word is used in the New Testament, eight times it describes the character of God, whose kindness leads us to repentance,[3] who out of His incomparable riches and His kindness gave us salvation in Christ.[4]

In English, the word *kind* comes from the root "kin." It originally meant to treat others as kin, as relatives. I think, therefore, that this attribute in our life is one so descriptive of all of our human relationships—that we bring people in and treat them as family.

An unkind person is hostile and punitive or indifferent. An unkind person reduces life to a set of rules: "If you keep the rules, everything will be all right. But I don't have to have mercy upon you if you don't keep the rules." Kindness does not reduce life to a set of rules. Kindness shows compassion even to those who break the rules.

Someone may even be faithful to God's rules and not have God's heart. That was Jonah's basic problem—he didn't have kindness. Kindness speaks of warmth in our human relationships. "Be kind and compassionate to one another, forgiving each other, just as in Christ God forgave you."[5]

GOODNESS

The sixth fruit of the Spirit is goodness. For some people, *good* means average. Goodness in the Bible is a very worthy trait. It describes a person in whom there is no deterioration, decay or rottenness. A person of goodness is clean and wholesome. What you see is what you get.

FAITHFULNESS

Faithfulness, the seventh fruit of the Spirit, also flows out of the others. Faith or faithfulness is the only fruit also listed as a gift. In the Greek, the same word is used for the gift of faith as the fruit. But the Greeks had a way of using the same word for either faith or faithfulness. So in the English translation, the word comes across as *faithfulness*. And faithfulness, likewise, flows out of God's character.

God is faithful to strengthen and protect us from the evil one.[6] God is faithful in that He will not let us be tested beyond what we can bear.[7] We need to say these things to ourselves when we're tested seemingly beyond our strength. God is faithful. He knows where our limits are and when to intervene in our times of testing.

God is faithful to us even when we are not faithful to Him.[8] God is faithful to forgive.[9] God has made a covenant that if we abide in Him, He is going to present us in that final day of judgment acquitted in His presence, when we stand before eternal God. Jesus is going to allow no one to come and accuse us. Each of us has experienced those times when the personality of Christ has not flowed through us as completely as it ought. But Jesus is going to be faithful to present us faultless before Him on that day.

A faithful person can be relied upon. Their word is good. They don't need a contract. When they make a commitment on the phone, or make an appointment, or accept an obligation, they can be counted on. A faithful person lives with fixed beliefs. There are things a person of faith knows are true and will never deny. A faithful person can successfully deal with obstacles. Sometimes faithfulness and faith call us to remove the obstacles, and other times faithfulness requires us to tunnel through them. A faithful person sticks with commitments regardless of feelings. A faithful person can be content with God's approval even if human approval isn't forthcoming.

GENTLENESS

The eighth fruit of the Spirit is gentleness. This is a difficult word to translate. At various times, it's translated as *meek*. It's used in three different ways in the

Greek language. First, it is used to describe the person who is not extreme—who is not on the one hand a miser or the other hand spends every nickel that comes in. This person is balanced.

Another way this word is used is of a wild horse that has been broken. Now, its energies have been channeled. That wild horse may be said to be disciplined. This doesn't mean it was tame, passive or lacking spunk, but rather that all the spunk has now been channeled for a purpose.

Then, there is a third definition of the word: gentleness. Balanced and disciplined people have a gentleness in their lifestyle. Jesus said, "I am gentle and humble in heart."[10] He certainly was not a passive, weak person. He had a strong personality but was gentle—with children, with women, and with His disciples.

This is a trait that is very helpful when people disagree with us. It's also helpful to be gentle in response to people who correct us. It's helpful to be gentle when people fail us. In Galatians 6:1, Paul said that when someone fails, falls into sin, we're to restore them in a spirit of gentleness. We're not to have a harsh attitude toward them.

SELF-CONTROL

The ninth fruit of the Spirit is self-control. This comes from the Greek, from which we derive terms like *democracy*. It relates to power. Theocracy is power to God. Democracy is power to the people. The term describes a person who is strong and in control. 1 Corinthians 9:25 speaks of the athlete. Here, Paul is speaking of a person who takes on disciplines, especially spiritual disciplines, which are a struggle at times to live with. Prayer is not easy. Studying the Scriptures is not easy; it can even be agonizing. Giving ourself to the Lord's work in any significant way involves development of character and training. Self-controlled people don't relinquish their happiness into the hands of someone else. They find strength in themselves through God's help.

FRUITFUL CHRISTIAN LIVING

When I was a little boy living in northwest China, we didn't get fresh fruit and vegetables. I loved oranges. Somehow, we'd gotten an orange and I saved the seeds to plant an orange tree so I could have oranges on a regular basis. I put some dirt in a little clay pot, put the seeds in it, and then put it by the stove. It was bitterly cold, and I knew I had to keep it warm. I really expected that within a few months, I'd have a tree growing out of my potted plant with oranges falling off of it. I'd watch it every day and nothing happened. I'd water it faithfully, but nothing ever grew. I think as Pentecostals we often want things to happen instantly. But the fruit of the Spirit tends to be more developmental. The development of fruit in all of the disciples was a growth process. It did not happen immediately. Peter did not become the rock overnight. It happened over time.

I see the fruit of the Spirit as sequential in development, much like the locks on a canal. A canal operates to move ships into a closed space called a lock. One body of water is lower than the next body of water they're moving to. Gradually, by the ship going uphill or down-hill, it moves through a sequence of locks. Each of the locks the ship moves through fills up with water and floats the ship higher. Slowly, it moves into the next lock and goes on.

I think developing the fruit of the Spirit is like that. Beginning with love, we progress until we've moved all the way through and come at last to that hardest of all to develop—the fruit of self-control.

The fruit of the Spirit tells us God is far more concerned with who we are than what we're doing. If you're looking for God's will for your life, don't look first of all at where God wants you to go, or even what God wants you to do. Look first of all at what God wants you to be. Probably 99 percent of knowing the will of God is being the person God wants you to be. Because if you are that person, you can go anywhere and do anything and you'll be guided by God and in His will.

I'm corresponding with a prisoner in California who is serving a life sentence for murder. During early childhood, his mom was a vibrant Christian and his dad also followed the Lord, although not as ebulliently as his wife. When the mom was in her late twenties, she got cancer and passed away within three months, leaving her husband with three small children. He turned extremely bitter against God and life. We did everything to try and help him, but he wouldn't listen. He remarried a woman he didn't love, whom he verbally abused. She also had a son by her first marriage. I heard they divorced, and their kids grew up, all in trouble with the juvenile system. This young man I'm corresponding with was the driver in a robbery that involved a murder and was sentenced to life. Thankfully, he came to Christ while in prison. All the trauma spiritually and emotionally could have been avoided had the father let the fruit of the Spirit grow in his life during his time of worst adversity.

The fruit of the Spirit allows us to take the high ground, rather than let somebody else's bitterness and anger get into us. There's no room in the Spirit-filled life for impoliteness, curtness, nastiness, self-pity or self-promotion. The fruit is designed to get all of those things out of our life. It often grows in adversity. This is the opposite of fruit in the natural sense.

When there is a chill, fruit freezes. If the weather is bad, a tree cannot survive. But the great thing about the fruit of the Spirit is that nothing can kill the development of Christ's personality within our life. Christ's personality grows in all kinds of temperatures, atmospheres and circumstances. The fruit of the Lord's personality is shown even to the point of martyrdom. Consider Stephen, who experienced a one-time gift as he was about to have his life extinguished. He responded with the love of Christ to those who were stoning him. He said, "Do not hold this sin against them."[11]

Revelation 22:1,2 points us to the future age when, in that eternal city of God, there will be a river running down the main street—a river called the river of the water of life. On either side of that river is the tree of life, changing fruit for every one of the twelve months of the year. I think this symbolically describes that where the life of God is present, there you will have the full and rich variety of the fruit of God.

I suggest we apply that picture of Revelation into our life now. When Christ's life is living in us, we will see the wonderful sight of His life-giving water bringing fruit to our own life. The great thing about fruit is that it's no good if it's just left on the tree. Fruit is meant to be eaten. This is how we are to be in our relationships with one another. God wants to make us delicious—delicious to the people we are living with. If we'll let Christ's personality be developed in our life, people who know us well will have a satisfying experience partaking of our life. This is why it's contradictory to be a crabby, mean or cantankerous Christian.

Fruit is meant to be tasted. The Scriptures tell us, "Taste and see that the Lord is good."[12] And we might add that the Lord wants us to be His tasty fruit in the world.

The gifts of the Spirit come to us through the miraculous endowment of God's Spirit. Some of them may also be developmental. The baptism in the Spirit happens often in a moment. But the fruit of the Spirit grows as we continue to sink our roots down in Christ. The key to developing fruit is to abide in Christ. "If a man remains in me and I in him, he will bear much fruit."[13]

_____

[1] Romans 5:3

[2] Ephesians 4:26

[3] Romans 2:4

[4] Ephesians 2:7

[5] Ephesians 4:32

[6] 2 Thessalonians 3:3

[7] 1 Corinthians 10:13

[8] 2 Timothy 2:11–13

[9] 1 John 1:9

[10] Matthew 11:29

[11] Acts 7:60

[12] Psalm 34:8

[13] John 15:5

CHAPTER SIX

THE GIFTS OF THE SPIRIT

THERE ARE
DIFFERENT KINDS
of GIFTS, *but the*
SAME SPIRIT....
ALL THESE ARE
the WORK *of* ONE
and the SAME SPIRIT.

—1 Corinthians 12:4,11

THE CHURCH IS IN THE WORLD TO FULFILL THE MISSION OF THE HEAD OF THE CHURCH. If we want to discover what the Church is about, we must know what Jesus is about. Jesus came in flesh with these four purposes: to glorify God, to evangelize and save the lost, to make disciples, and to meet human need. Where the Head of the Church goes, the Body that belongs to the Head must follow.

The gifts of the Spirit are given to fulfill the mission of the Church. The gifts do not exist for us to stand back and view them in amazement—especially those gifts with supernatural connotations. Rather, the gifts are designed to fulfill a mission. The gifts He gives to the body of Christ are designed to accomplish that mission.

JESUS AND THE CHURCH

All the gifts, with the exception of tongues, were evidenced in Jesus' ministry. The key to understanding spiritual gifts, then, is to see them as a perpetuation of Jesus' ministry. In Acts 1:1, Luke said, "In my former book, Theophilus, I wrote about all that Jesus began to do and to teach." What's so striking about that introduction to Acts is that it follows Luke's first volume (the Gospel of Luke), in which he traces the ministry of Jesus from His conception through His ascent into heaven.

Luke said as he began his second volume—the history of the Church—that the first volume only contains that which Jesus *began* to do and to teach. All that is described in the Book of Acts is the continuing life and ministry of Jesus, which the Spirit makes possible. It isn't so much the Church ministering as it is Jesus ministering through His Church. The gifts resident in Him are now being expressed through His body.

Ephesians 4:8 helps us understand and put these gifts in the context of Christ's gifts to His Church: "When he ascended on high, he led captives in his train [a courtly kingly procession of which there are attendants who are following after him] and gave gifts to men." This is a quotation from Psalm 68:18 with one exception—in Ephesians 4, Paul completely changed a word, which renders a different meaning in the quotation.

Psalm 68:18 speaks of the kingly reign of Jesus and says, "When you ascended on high, you led captives in your train; you received gifts from men." That's logical. A person who conquers sits on a throne and people bring him gifts. That's what Psalm 68 says. But in quoting this passage in the New Testament, Paul—by the Spirit—gives a deeper revelation of the work of Jesus. He said when Jesus ascended on high and had behind Him a train of captives (we are that train who have been captured by His love), He turned around and didn't simply receive gifts, He *gave* gifts. Then Paul goes on to tell us that the gifts of the Spirit with which the Church functions are really the gifts Jesus has given to His body.

And God gives good gifts. He begins by giving us the gift of eternal life.[1] He then gives us the gift of the Holy Spirit.[2] Once we've been given these initial gifts of entry into the Christian life, we have a great variety of gifts the Spirit brings to us personally and to the church as a whole because of Christ.

Perhaps if you've ever heard a description of the gifts of the Spirit, you have had that description limited to the nine gifts described from 1 Corinthians 12. That was my thinking for many years as I looked at the Scripture—that there are nine gifts of the Spirit. But I think a more serious study of Scripture has to take into account three major "gift passages" in the New Testament—gifts for the glorification of God, the reaching of the lost, the discipling of the found, and the serving of human need.

First, Romans 12:6–8 lists seven gifts, often called motivational gifts. Second, the nine gifts in 1 Corinthians 12:7–11 are sometimes called the spiritualities (spiritual gifts). In 1 Corinthians 12:7–11, they're not referred to as gifts but as *pneumatika*, from the Greek *pneuma* which means "spirit." The people in the Corinthian church had a lot of carnalities, so Paul is saying, "In opposition to the carnalities, let me talk to you about the spiritualities." The third set of gifts—ministry gifts—are listed in 1 Corinthians 12:27–31. Ephesians 4:11–13 describes additional ministry gifts.

Motivational gifts are those gifts that explain the motivation of the people in the Body to minister to one another. We go past that to spiritual gifts, often called the *charismata*, which means "graces." They are grace gifts of God. Then there are ministry gifts—gifts that apply to an office in the church. I'd like to supply the gift catalog of all these gifts without repeating any.

MOTIVATIONAL GIFTS (Romans 12:6–8)

Prophecy: When most people think of the word *prophecy*, they think of someone standing up in a service and uttering something like, "I, the Lord thy God, say unto thee . . ." Sometimes, unless we hear a person use such a formula, we'll leave the service assuming there has been no prophetic word spoken by the Lord.

What is a prophet? We find an excellent definition in 1 Samuel 9:9. Before men of God were called prophets, they were called seers, ones who saw. What did the prophets see? The prophets always saw the world and people through God's eyes. Primarily that seeing was twofold in nature. It was intuitive, that is, it looked into the heart of a person and read that person's needs and perhaps sins in the light of God's Word, and then addressed God's Word to that particular need. Prophets were also prophetic in the sense that we are used to the word—they indicated events that were to come.

Prophecy always arises out of a true seeing of current conditions. It says, "If these conditions continue, this is where they are going to lead you, and God is going to either judge you or bless you, depending upon how you address and correct the situation." Prophecy involves both forth-telling—declaring the Word of God now to our heart, and it also may involve foretelling, that is, telling of the future.

1 Corinthians 14:3 indicates that prophecy builds up, encourages and consoles believers. To nonbelievers, 1 Corinthians 14:24,25 says that prophecy convicts and

brings a person to the point of making a decision to follow Christ.

The gift of prophecy is to be earnestly sought by all believers. When Moses found out that two more were prophesying in the camp without credentials, he said, "Would that all the Lord's people were prophets."[3] Like Moses, we should also say, "Would that we all would come to know God and His Word so intimately that when the occasion arises, we can speak out God's Word with authority."

Service: The gift of service involves practical ministry to needs. Jesus epitomized this gift when, on the eve of His passion, He took a towel and washed His disciples' feet. He demonstrated, through His practical service, the ministry of love.

Notice that nowhere do the Scriptures say the gift of prophecy is greater than the gift of serving, or serving greater than prophecy. Both are vital components. The body of Christ needs people who speak the Word of God and also people who serve with the Spirit and the heart of Jesus.

Teaching: While the prophet will speak to the moment, teachers are systematic and strive for accuracy. Luke was a masterful teacher. You can pick this up in his writings. The gift of the Spirit rested upon him. He described in Luke 1:3 how he had followed all things accurately and served to set down in order the things concerning Jesus. Apollos, in Acts 18:24,25, "was a learned man, with a thorough knowledge of the Scriptures. He had been instructed in the way of the

Lord, and he spoke with great fervor and taught about Jesus accurately."

A great quality of a teacher, like Apollos, is to be teachable as well. Apollos received the teaching of Priscilla and Aquila,[4] and became even more effective in his ministry. Because of his gift of teaching, he built up believers and confounded unbelievers. We need to be taught and have set before us God's full counsel. The body of Jesus Christ suffers whenever teaching is not accurate.

Encouragement: Another speaking gift, the gift of exhortation, is literally encouragement. It's the Greek word for "one called alongside to help." The gift of prophecy, the gift of teaching, and the gift of encouragement all interrelate. The prophet, the teacher and the exhorter (or encourager) depend upon different ways to get their message across. The prophet depends upon his or her interaction with the Spirit of God and with the Word. The teacher depends upon a thorough mastery of the subject in order to address it. The exhorter depends upon a need to arise that he or she can address to help encourage and inspire people.

Barnabas was an encourager. His story is told for us in Acts 11 with the founding of the church at Antioch. Barnabas went and saw what God was doing among the Gentiles and ministered to the assembled believers. But he knew the congregation at Antioch could not thrive long on an exhortative ministry. They needed the ministry of a teacher as well. So Barnabas went to Tarsus and found Saul. The Scripture says they taught the believers—and the word *teaching* comes into the account once Paul arrived on the scene.

Barnabas was the kind of person who could put his arms around an individual or a congregation and minister in such a way that they would be inspired. The Church needs people who have the ministry of encouragement, both to the church as a corporate body and to us as individuals. We need people to put their arms around us, encourage us and inspire us.

Giving: In each of the gifts, there are dimensions of that gift that are universal to all believers. To say that some have the gift of giving does not mean that others do not give. Or to say that some have the gift of teaching does not mean that others should not teach. There is universality in each of the gifts, but there are gifts that have special application and refinement as we use them.

There are some members in the Body who have the unique gift of seeing and responding to needs. If you have the gift of giving, you need resources to give, whether it's time, finances or skills. The giver gives these willingly. He or she doesn't ever give begrudgingly, because God has given them a special delight in sharing for the benefit of the Body.

Leadership: Leadership is the ability given by the Spirit to help set a course of direction and unify people for the accomplishment of the work of the Lord. Leadership helps the body of Christ strive toward common ideals, and builds the community of the people of God into that which would delight the Spirit of the Lord. It helps people move to fulfill the objectives the

Lord has for them. There are all kinds of leaders. Servant leadership perhaps best describes the leadership the Spirit places in the Body.

Mercy: Paul concludes in Romans 12 with the gift of mercy. There are often critical needs when teaching or words of any kind cannot help. So we need the gift of mercy. When a person is terminally ill, it isn't the prophet or teacher or even exhorter who has the impact. It's the person who can show mercy, inspired by Christ's example.

Many in our society need the gift of mercy—not only the terminally ill, but also abused people, victims of AIDS, prisoners and outcasts. The Church is often too quick to pronounce judgment. We may recognize God judges sin but loves the sinner, yet we often weigh the first half of that equation too heavily. We must reach out with love and with compassion because people are won to Christ through love. The merciful person reaches out and administers the redemption and inner healing of Jesus Christ.

SPIRITUAL GIFTS (I Corinthians 12:7–11)

Wisdom: Wisdom is a trait of character, discipline and thought life. But it's also a special gift of the Spirit in which one speaks an utterance of wisdom. Jesus exhibited this gift in John 8:7 when His enemies confronted Him with the woman caught in adultery. They asked Him to judge her. He, with a word of wisdom, turned the whole situation on its head and said, "If any one of you is without sin, let him be the first to throw a stone at her."

That word of wisdom is also seen operating in the Early Church in Acts 15:13–21. The church is debating the matter of the inclusion of non-Jews into the body and James, the leader of the assembly, speaks a word of wisdom. It's especially important whenever we come to critical decision junctions in our lives—whether it's a decision of the local body of believers or a personal decision, that we be open to this particular gift.

Knowledge: The Spirit's gift of knowledge is not book learning or scholarly knowledge, but an utterance of divine knowledge. The person exercising this gift often knows God's Word in a deep way or knows something of immediate circumstances. The prophet Nathan knew that David had an affair with Bathsheba when no one else knew. Jesus had the gift of knowledge when He said to Nathaniel in John 1:48, "I saw you while you were still under the fig tree." He knew what Nathaniel was doing. Peter said to Ananaias, when he brought his dishonest offering, "You have not lied to men but to God."[5]

Faith: We're all called upon to have faith, but there's a special operation of the gift of faith that is a supernatural endowment by the Holy Spirit. It enables a person to believe for an extra demonstration of the power of God. There are some who have the gift of faith that causes faith to arise in another believer, or even in a whole group of people, to accomplish something. A person with the gift of faith grasps the vision of what God wants to bring to pass and confidently lives and works to see it take place. Faith helps believers continue in trial.[6]

I think back to when we would encourage people in our church to find a place of ministry and the gifts that go with it will come. We started the Royal Family Kids

Camp back in 1985. That began as a vision from associate pastor Wayne Tesch who wanted to do a camp for abused children. He said it would cost about five thousand dollars, which was our total weekly income at the time. But he felt it was from the Lord. So we presented the need to the congregation and a little over five thousand dollars came in. I will never forget the night we commissioned the volunteers who were going to work with the kids. While we were praying, someone began a prophetic word. At the time, I didn't recognize it as Scripture, but it was from Isaiah 58:11,12: "You will be like a well-watered garden, like a spring whose waters never fail . . . you will be called Repairer of Broken Walls, Restorer of Streets with Dwellings." It was an incredible word.

Today, there are about 160 camps with more than six thousand kids involved annually. Alumni from those early years now tell their testimonies of how that one week changed their lives. Wayne had a gift of faith—faith that God could bring this to pass. And a prophetic gift was also exercised, which brought confirmation that it was a ministry the Lord wanted to use. So in that instance, there was a blending of gifts— prophecy and faith.

We often identify the gift of faith as functioning only with those who see immediate results. But there are two dimensions of faith. There's the faith that sees immediate results, then there's the gift of faith that perseveres when there is no immediate sign. In this case, the believer continues to faithfully trust that what God has spoken, He'll bring to pass.

My uncle, Victor Plymire, is an example of a person who functioned with the gift of faith. He served on the border of China and Tibet for sixteen years before baptizing his first convert. Nevertheless, he believed that God had called him there and would accomplish His purposes.

Adoniram Judson went as a missionary apostle to Burma in the early 1800s. It was seven years before someone came to the Lord. When he died, he left behind seven thousand believers and had established sixty-three churches. The body of Christ in Burma (now Myanmar) today is a direct flowering of his gift of faith.

Gifts of Healings: Both *gifts* and *healings* are in the plural in the Greek. There are different ways healing is administered—through the laying on of hands, through speaking an authoritative word, or through anointing with oil. There are varieties of gifts and varieties of healings—physical healings, emotional healings, spiritual healings, gradual healings, instant healings. There are those who fraudulently claim to have a so-called miracle ministry. But there are many others whom the Spirit has used in powerful ways.

When I first interviewed Pastor Mung in northwest China, he was eighty years old. He had reopened a church at seventy-five with thirty old people. Five years later, it had grown to about 1,500 believers. He said, "Jesus Christ is the same yesterday, today, and forever, and we pray a lot." He then went on to describe how healings had taken place. A Communist party official's wife was at home, dying of cancer. They secretly called

138 • LIVING IN THE SPIRIT

for Pastor Mung to come and pray for her, and God raised her up. It became a tremendous testimony in the community.

There are many people whose faith functions in one particular area. Some have a gift for praying for people who have cancer and others for people who have paralysis. Some pray for those who are possessed of evil spirits and others for deliverance from alcohol or drug addiction. There are many needs for healing and varying gifts of healing to be administered.

Miracles: Miracles are distinguished from healings in that miracles include a demonstration of God's power in an unusual measure. They especially relate to miracles in the realm of nature, such as Jesus' feeding of the five thousand or His miracles that involved the resurrection of the dead.

The gift of miracles vindicates the name of God. Elijah faced the prophets of Baal and saw a miracle that vindicated God's name. The gift of miracles may deliver God's people from the hands of an enemy, as with Moses and the Israelites. A miracle may provide for someone in desperate need, as with Elijah and the widow at Zarephath.

Discerning of Spirits: This gift allows people to distinguish whether or not a person brings a spiritual message from God. Paul warned the pastors at Ephesus to distinguish between those who come as wolves in sheep's clothing and those who bear a true message from God.[7] Discernment is needed to determine whether or not a person and message are sent from God.

This discernment distinguishes between outward appearances and inward realities. In Acts 8, Simon Magus outwardly appeared to be an earnest seeker. But Peter's gift of discernment saw him as a fraud who wanted the gift of the Spirit for his own advancement. The discernment of spirits is needed to distinguish the Spirit of God from the spirit of man or an evil spirit. Some people erroneously attribute sin or illness to an evil spirit. But not every work of the flesh should be categorized as a demonic manifestation.

Tongues: In 1 Corinthians 12, the gift of tongues differs from personal tongues. It refers to tongues that occur in a public setting. In this case, control is necessary. A person who speaks out in tongues must pray to interpret. There must be no more than two or three in a service who speak in tongues for the Body. And, they must speak at an appropriate time and in an appropriate way. We know from Acts 2, Romans 8:26 and 1 Corinthians 14:2 that tongues is directed to God as the language of praise, intercession or prayer.

Interpretation of Tongues: When an utterance in tongues is given in a public worship service, the Scripture requires an interpretation. But, an interpretation is not necessarily a literal translation. For example, sometimes what happens in the Spirit is very visual. When I am giving a prophetic word, I have a very visual experience of seeing God unfold a picture before me. You interpret a painting differently than you interpret a written text. Communication from God is not merely verbal, but sometimes needs to be expressed in words.

This is one reason why sometimes an interpretation is shorter or longer than the utterance in tongues.

MINISTRY GIFTS
(1 Corinthians 12:27–31; Ephesians 4:11–13)

Apostle: An apostle, in the technical New Testament sense, is an eyewitness of Jesus who has been commissioned by Him to lay the foundation of the Church. Paul said in 2 Corinthians 12:12, that signs, wonders and miracles mark an apostle. An apostle has a supernatural ministry. We might extend the idea of an apostle to someone today who goes into an area where the Church does not exist, and through whose labor and ministry the Church is brought into being. Many missionaries function in an apostolic way.

Helps: Helps is a special ability to invest talents in the life and ministry of others in the Body, thus enabling that person to increase their effectiveness and their own spiritual gifts. Dr. Raymond Ortlund of Renewal Ministries called people who have the gift of helps, "the glorious company of the stretcher bearers." Remember in Mark 2 the four who brought the paralytic on the stretcher? For that man to get to Jesus, it required somebody who had the ministry of helps. They had to help him get to Jesus.

Administration: Called "governments" in the King James Version, the Greek word here means someone who steers the course and makes sure that everybody is bending toward accomplishing that course. People with the gift of administration are able to articulate a vision and unify the people of God to accomplish it.

I mentioned earlier the gift of leadership. How does it differ from the gift of administration? The gift of administration involves efficiency; it involves setting out a task and mapping how to accomplish the task. It involves pulling in all the loose ends and taking care of all the details, and making sure the ship is running on course. It's the job of a helmsman rather than a captain. Not all administrators are leaders, and not all leaders are administrators. The leader needs the administrator and the administrator needs the leader. We shouldn't saddle people with things that aren't their calling.

Evangelist: The evangelist has the special gift of sharing the gospel in such a way that men and women respond to follow Jesus. All of us are called to evangelism—to be witnesses. But there are some in the body of Christ who are given the special equipment of being an evangelist. When they get up to testify or witness, people are always coming to the Lord. This doesn't excuse the rest of us from being witnesses, but it does recognize that there are those who especially have that gift.

Pastor: The pastor assumes the responsibility of the spiritual welfare of God's people. The word *pastor* literally means shepherd, one who looks out for a flock.

FOUR ADDITIONAL GIFTS
(1 Corinthians 7:7; 1 Corinthians 13:3; 1 Peter 4:9)

Other references perhaps describe four additional gifts.

Celibacy: In 1 Corinthians 7:7, celibacy is called a

charisma, a spiritual gift. Celibacy is the spiritual gift of being able to remain single and not suffer undue sexual temptation. Paul emphasized that in singleness, the believer has more time to give to the Lord, to His work and to His people.

Voluntary Poverty: In 1 Corinthians 13:3, Paul talked about giving up worldly goods: "If I give all I possess to the poor." Here is a person who is given by the Spirit the unique ability to empty him- or herself of all assets for the care of others.

Martyrdom: Paul said in 1 Corinthians 13:3, "If I . . . surrender [or give] my body to the flames." The history of the Church is replete with men and women who received this gift and offered their life as a testimony to the ages.

Hospitality: 1 Peter 4:9 says, "Offer hospitality to one another." This phrase is immediately followed by an admonition to use your spiritual gifts. I submit to you that if the admonition to use your spiritual gifts is immediately preceded by a teaching on hospitality, then the apostle Peter is considering hospitality—the special reaching out to others—as a gift of the Spirit.

TEN TRUTHS OF THE GIFTS

Let me quickly summarize the use of the gifts.

(1) The gifts are for Christians. You can't receive the gifts or function in these gifts—which are meant to glorify God, to build up the Body, to save the lost, to serve human need—unless you first receive the gift of salvation. The gifts are meant to flourish among those who are baptized in the Spirit. Spirit baptism plunges a

person into new dimensions of intimacy with God and empowerment for witness.

(2) The gifts are given for the benefit of the Body and for Christ's work in the world. No gift is more glamorous than another. People tend to especially consider miracles and healing as being more outstanding than the other gifts. The gifts are not given that we might be bigger stars, but that we might be better servants.

(3) The gifts should never be divorced from love. Paul told us in 1 Corinthians 14:1 to "follow the way of love and eagerly desire spiritual gifts." 1 Corinthians 13 is a reminder in the middle of a section dealing with spiritual gifts that we are to walk in the way of love.

(4) The gifts should not be confused with spirituality. Some people measure their spirituality on the basis of their gifts. The gifts often have little to do with spirituality. They have to do with getting the work of the Lord done. There are going to be people, as Jesus said in Matthew 7, who stand before Him on that Day and talk about the wonderful work they did for Christ. And the Lord is going to say, "I never knew you." I've known people who have had real gifts of the Spirit in operation but who have been apostate in their life and character. Once given, the gifts are irrevocable. They can still function. The gifts are not to be confused with spirituality, so we shouldn't follow after people simply because they have gifts.

(5) The gifts are often matched with natural inclinations and abilities. People who have a tender heart are often the ones functioning in the gift of mercy. People

who are highly organized are often functioning in the gift of teaching. People who are naturally happy and glad are usually functioning in the gift of exhortation.

The gifts aren't natural inclinations, but they often build from a base of natural inclinations.

(6) The gifts tend to be developmental in nature. That's why we're told in 1 Corinthians 14 to perfect the gifts. Jesus said, in Luke 19, that to him who has, more will be given. We need to continue using the gifts to see them developed. All the gifts are this way.

(7) The gifts are not proprietary. They are not *my* gifts, or, I'll use them whenever *I* want to. They are for the Body.

(8) The use of each gift will be confirmed by the body of Christ. There's no true ongoing function of a gift unless it has ratification from other believers. That's why we need to encourage and affirm one another.

(9) Individual exercise of a gift emerges from a combination of desire, prayer and need. What are the desires that God has placed in my heart? What comes to me while I'm praying? What need is the Holy Spirit calling me to address? It's when we consider the matrix of these things—desire, prayer and need—that God begins to individually appoint us to our particular mission, our unique calling.

(10) The last thing about the gifts is perhaps surprising: only a few of them occur in a church service. If you look carefully at the gifts of the Spirit as they occur in the Book of Acts, the gifts mostly occur in the market-place. The majority of them occur in everyday service to

Christ or in the functioning of the Body outside of the worship service, in ministry to the world.

Some assume that when we come to a service, the Holy Spirit is limited to working in that service. When the church is dispersed the rest of the week, some think of the Spirit as inactive, waiting to work until we assemble again. But the Spirit wants to work throughout His body every day of the week. He seeks to bring His people into wholeness. We need—the Church needs— the gifts of the Spirit.

———————

[1] Romans 6:23
[2] Acts 2:38
[3] Numbers 11:29, NASB
[4] Acts 18:26
[5] Acts 5:6
[6] Hebrews 11:30–40
[7] Acts 20:28,29

CHAPTER SEVEN

DECENTLY
AND IN
ORDER

THE SPIRITS *of*
PROPHETS ARE
SUBJECT *to the*
CONTROL *of*
PROPHETS....
EVERYTHING
SHOULD BE DONE
in a FITTING *and*
ORDERLY WAY.

—1 Corinthians 14:32,40

THROUGHOUT ITS HISTORY, THE ASSEMBLIES OF GOD HAS HELD UNWAVERINGLY to the full expression of spiritual gifts in our churches. That openness to the ministry of God's Spirit in our midst is a driving factor behind the continuing growth of our Fellowship worldwide. But, as with any biblical doctrine, human interpretation and expression can interfere with and diminish divine purpose.

One of the problems experienced within the Pentecostal movement in general, and within the Assemblies of God as well, is a lack of adequate instruction on the correct expression of spiritual gifts and a lack of correction when spiritual gifts are misused. Too often in such an environment, misuse of the gifts leads to lack of use, and congregations can become Pentecostal in name only.

As a pastor, I wanted to encourage everyone in our church to be open to the move of the Spirit in each of their lives for the benefit of all. To that end, I taught on spiritual gifts and regularly reminded our people that they were all vessels for ministry. When a vocal gift occurred in the congregation, I took time to explain what had happened because in every service we had people who were not believers. I would always explain that we invested much prayer and planning into the service, but we were open to whatever the Holy Spirit desired to do through His body in response to those needs only He could see. A prophetic word, tongues, interpretation of tongues, a word of wisdom, a word of knowledge—any and all of these were the Holy Spirit's divinely orchestrated means of addressing specific needs in people's lives that day.

Spiritual gifts are to glorify Christ, edify believers, and serve as a positive witness to nonbelievers. With those purposes in view, the commands in 1 Corinthians 14 explaining how gifts are to be expressed decently and in order take on special urgency. There can be no room for gifts exercised inappropriately or for personality spotlighting under the guise of gift expression.

I see two major differences between the Assemblies of God of a generation or two ago and the Assemblies of God today. First, we have many larger churches where the sheer numbers of people present call for more careful controls from the platform in the order of a service. Second, we have a culture that has largely shifted from participation to observation. We have many believers who are content to be mere spectators in a service. Within this environment, one of the greatest challenges a pastor will face is the dual responsibility of nurturing the full Pentecostal life of the church while curtailing any abuses or misuses of gifts.

Pastors and congregations who work together to promote the widest possible expression of spiritual gifts will see their churches reach the greatest potential for growth and community outreach. There must be deliberate planning to help the congregation understand that each service is a participatory event. Just as the pastor and the leadership are to be praying, the congregation also needs to be praying that the Holy Spirit will find receptive vessels for whatever form of ministry He chooses to use.

The pastor and congregation who agree in their commitment to spiritual gift expression will also agree on the need for development of those gifts. Often, the person who begins to exercise a spiritual gift needs encouragement to mature in that and other gifts. A church should foster the development of spiritual gifts without squelching their expression.

The acid test of spirituality is whether or not a person can receive correction. The person who is unreceptive or even defensive because he or she is corrected in the use of a spiritual gift is really demonstrating a lack of preparation to be used in that gift expression in the first place. By the same token, a pastor who might read the guidance offered in this chapter and take offense should do some soul-searching. Is he or she truly prepared to encourage the kind of gift expression in the congregation that will bring about the fullest possible spiritual life?

At some point, every pastor confronts a seeming paradox of Pentecost: if a person is demonstrating a genuine spiritual gift, how is it possible to misuse that gift? Scripture doesn't leave us in the dark on this matter. Paul, in writing to the Corinthian church about the use of spiritual gifts in a worship gathering, made it clear: "The spirits of prophets are subject to the control of prophets."[1] In other words, the Holy Spirit gives us the ability to speak in tongues, to interpret tongues, to prophesy—but He does not force us to blurt out those gifts. He expects His gifts to be exercised with discretion and maturity.

The test that I believe should be applied to all spiritual gifts is simple and threefold: (1) Does it glorify Jesus

Christ? (2) Does it edify the saints? and (3) Is it a good witness to nonbelievers? If it fails any one of those tests, it probably is out of order.

"But wait a minute," someone might object, "if something is bringing glory to Jesus Christ, don't the saints and nonbelievers have a problem if they can't receive that?"

Not really. An utterance that simply proclaims praise to Jesus is not truly glorifying to Him if it is disruptive, compromises the spiritual life and growth of the redeemed, or puts a roadblock in the path of those needing redemption. Jesus is truly glorified when His church worships in unity, creating an environment where the Holy Spirit can powerfully convict and transform the lost.

TONGUES-LASHING

I remember a woman in the church I pastored who was certainly godly and committed to prayer. But she had a knack for compromising key moments in services. Often, it would be at the close of a sermon as I was prepared to invite people to respond.

She would erupt like a volcano. In a shrill and earsplitting pitch, she would let loose. She would speak in rapid-fire tongues at the top of her lungs and follow up that utterance with an equally screeching interpretation.

I had taught our people that you don't have to use King James English when you give a spiritual gift. Offer your message in your normal tone of voice. Don't announce a word from the Lord with a "Yea, yea" formula. But this sister was using all the King James

English she knew, proclaiming each message with "Yea, yea" or "Hear ye the word of the Lord," and delivering everything at a strident crescendo.

I was a young minister then, she was older, and I wasn't very confrontational. She absolutely wrecked the service three or four times and people were coming to me. They said, "You know, George, we've been bringing friends, and they walk away from here scratching their heads saying 'What in the world?' We can't keep bringing people if you're going to allow this to happen."

I knew I had to deal with it. So the next Sunday morning that it happened, I approached her after service. "I need to talk to you this afternoon, before the Sunday evening service," I said.

She and her husband came to my office. We sat down and I said, "You know, I have three tests for spiritual gifts: Does it glorify the Lord? Does it edify or build up the believer? And third, does it positively influence those who don't know Christ who are in the service?"

So far, so good.

I said, "I know you're a woman of prayer, and I don't doubt at all your spiritual integrity, but the way you are exercising the gift with a shrill tone of voice almost makes the service about you and not anyone else. You've so dominated this in the last few Sundays that there have not been other gifts functioning from other people." I explained that I did not feel what was happening was glorifying the Lord, edifying the saints, or effectively witnessing to nonbelievers. I invited her to be in our church awhile and learn our understanding of how the gifts operate.

"We'll evaluate this and sit down and talk again," I promised. "At an appropriate time, I'll give you an indication of when I release you to do this. But I'm going to ask you now, not to exercise this anymore."

She looked at me unfazed and said, "This is not me. This is the Holy Spirit who comes on me. It's not me."

I had not thought of that response, but I shot up a quick prayer for guidance and offered her two answers.

"Number one," I said, "the next time you feel the Holy Spirit telling you to do this, you tell the Holy Spirit that you can't do it, that the pastor has forbidden you. We have plenty of qualified people in this congregation to whom the Spirit can go, and you ask the Spirit to go to one of them."

"Second," I said, "if there's any fallout on the Judgment Day for your disobeying the Spirit, I'll take the blame for it."

You can always tell how spiritually mature a person is by whether they receive correction or not. Within a few days that woman and her husband left the church. But the church had peace and was multiplied!

ATTACK AT THE ALTAR

When I had served at that church just a few years, we went through a merger with another congregation. The church that joined us had dwindled over the years until just sixty people or so were meeting in a sanctuary that could hold five hundred. In the course of that merger, I inherited a deacon.

When we had altar time, this brother would pray at

the top of his voice. Nobody else could really concentrate in prayer. Even I struggled to string together my thoughts in prayer because I was forced to hear every word this man was yelling.

It was becoming a disaster for the congregation. I would call people forward to the altar in response to a real need God had brought to life in the message or throughout the service. People would come forward in obedient response to the Holy Spirit's prompting. But there was always a sense of tension because everyone knew this brother was going to go up as well.

He wasn't exercising a spiritual gift; it was just personal prayer. But his behavior reflected the abuses people make of the gifts of the Spirit. He would just yell at the top of his lungs about whatever was burdening his heart with no thought to what the Spirit wanted to accomplish in the people around him.

I went to him privately. "You know," I said, "I've noticed that at the altar time you really cry loudly to the Lord. I know your heart is sincere, but the loudness of your prayer, the way you're praying, is preventing other people from praying. They can't concentrate on what their own prayers are."

I gently asked him to lower his voice when he prayed in order to make room for other people to pray. I spoke of the benefit to our church when everyone could pray in concert.

He took tremendous offense at what I said. At first he quit coming to the altar; then he left the church altogether.

I feel badly whenever I lose people. At the same

time, I am determined never to allow anyone to hijack for themselves what the Holy Spirit desires to do among the congregation. I'm convinced a lot of the "spiritual" stuff that goes on in our churches is just self-indulgence.

TESTED AND "PROPHET-ABLE"

If you're going to have spiritual gifts operate, you must have wisdom accompanying that operation. Too often, pastors go in one of two extremes. Some are afraid to exert too much control. One reason why gifts die out in many of our churches is the abuses that arise through a lack of control. On the other hand, some pastors want to get through the program and not make room for gifts at all because they fear that some of the ways gifts might be expressed would be destructive to the life of the congregation.

It can be especially difficult to correct abuses when you have a smaller congregation. Family members are quick to defend the person corrected; even gentle correction can make someone feel alienated. But you still have to tackle it if you're going to have growth.

I was determined to protect the growth in my church. I was also determined there would be opportunity for verbal gifts, whether it was tongues, interpretation of tongues, or a prophetic word. When we began to get new people in the congregation, I asked that verbal exercise of the gifts be limited to people I knew were spiritually fruitful. If I did not know someone who was exercising a spiritual gift, I would intervene. It didn't happen a lot, but it happened several times.

Pastoral intervention does not have to be radical. "My brother, my sister, you're not familiar to us," I would say, "and I'd like for you to establish your walk in this congregation so we know of your life and ministry prior to your exercising a gift."

If the gift expressed was in order, I would always give an explanation, because at every service there would be people who had never seen that happen before.

"What you have just heard expressed," I would say, "is described for us in the Bible.[2] The Holy Spirit gives gifts, and among the gifts are tongues, interpretation, and prophecy."

I would explain how our church leadership put a great deal of planning into the service, but that on occasion the Holy Spirit, who knows our hearts, had a very pointed personal message to give to one or several in the congregation or sometimes to the entire congregation. "It may be something we hadn't thought of, we hadn't planned, we hadn't prayed for in the service," I would say. "The Spirit has not interrupted this service; He has particularized an agenda He has that we didn't see. This is the Lord's way of talking to your heart personally. You'll have to take that to your heart and assess it yourself."

With guidelines in place, our people learned what the uses of the gifts are. Prophecy, for example, is for correction, consolation and encouragement. A prophetic word can be an anointed sermon—a person speaking on behalf of God. A prophetic word from the congregation, when sensitively presented, can also accomplish valuable spiritual goals.

But if we throw guidelines aside, if we only accept as prophecy some sort of extemporaneous speech that happens unplanned or interrupts a service, I believe we are missing out on the full dimensionality of what exercising prophetic gifts is really all about. Guidelines, then, are intended to maximize what the Holy Spirit would accomplish among God's people. The true servant of God who desires to have the greatest impact for good on fellow members in the body of Christ and on the lost will not resent instruction or correction. He or she will partner with a pastor to ensure God's purposes are fulfilled in the church.

I pray that a new generation of church leadership will catch a vision for the vast spectrum of spiritual gift expression that has empowered the Church since its birth. I pray that congregations across our Fellowship will perform some prayerful soul-searching and identify anything that would hinder or in any way deform the pure and powerful use of the Holy Spirit's ministry.

As Paul said to the Corinthians, "The spirits of prophets are subject to the control of prophets. . . . Everything should be done in a fitting and orderly way."[3] When spiritual gifts are used properly and correctly, they produce powerful results in our churches.

---

[1] 1 Corinthians 14:32
[2] 1 Corinthians 12 through 14
[3] 1 Corinthians 14:32,40

CHAPTER EIGHT

THE WORK OF
THE SPIRIT

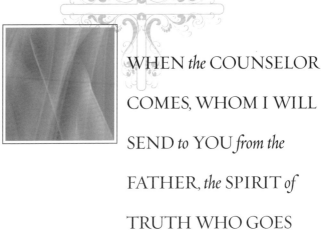

WHEN *the* COUNSELOR COMES, WHOM I WILL SEND *to* YOU *from the* FATHER, *the* SPIRIT *of* TRUTH WHO GOES OUT *from the* FATHER, HE WILL TESTIFY ABOUT ME.

—John 15:26

WE WERE IN THE MIDDLE OF CON-STRUCTING OUR NEW CHURCH FACILITIES. Our church offices were in trailers. One day a man walked in and told me a sob story you often hear if you are a pastor. The man was passing through town with his wife and babies and needed milk and food. Normally, I would have referred him on to the food bank that we participated in for indigents; but I felt the Spirit say to me, "Give him sixty dollars." I fought with that impression. We didn't have sixty dollars cash on hand in my office, but I had three twenty-dollar bills in my wallet. The impression grew stronger: "Give him the sixty dollars you have." Reluctantly, I pulled out my wallet, extracted the money and gave it to him.

As soon as he left, I thought to myself, *I am such a fool. I just blew sixty dollars that I couldn't afford to and this guy just conned me.* I left my office and decided to go to a lookout space in a building nearby to see if the man had gone in the direction he said he would. He did. But, I was still kicking myself. I wasn't gone from my trailer office for more than ten minutes, but when I returned there was a sealed envelope that had been dropped on my desk in those brief moments I had been away. I opened it. There were three twenty-dollar bills inside and a note that said, "Pastor, I believe that your shoes are starting to wear and I want you to use this to buy a new pair of shoes."

I thought, *How could that man have gotten back into the trailer?* But, I realized he hadn't because I had watched him all during that time. So, over the years I shared that story a few times with our congregation and even ventured a wonder if an angel had come and done that.

Finally, one of our widows came to me one day and said, "Pastor, I've heard you talk about the angel. I hate to disappoint you, but I was the one who put the money on your desk. I just wanted you to have new shoes."

That incident taught me several lessons. It reawakened in me the truth of Scripture, "It is more blessed to give than to receive." It also helped me realize that not every stranger that asks for help is a con artist. Obey the prompting of the Spirit.

The Holy Spirit has always been active. From the beginning of Scripture, we find the Spirit of God engaged in activity. The Spirit of God was moving upon the face of the waters.[1] Throughout the Old Testament, the Spirit's activity is frequently recorded. He would come upon people, such as judges, kings and prophets.

When the Spirit came upon someone, He stirred them to action. Often, you read that they crossed over, went up or down, spoke or defeated an enemy. When the Spirit comes, we respond with action because He is the One who generates the activity in the kingdom of God.

THE SPIRIT AND THE MINISTRY OF JESUS

Just as the Spirit was present in power upon Old Testament saints, we see the Spirit also at work in the life of Jesus. We cannot completely understand how the conception of Jesus took place by the Spirit.[2] Mary conceived Jesus by the Spirit. Similarly, on a spiritual level, the Spirit seeks to birth Jesus in each of our lives.

The Spirit descended upon Jesus bodily as a dove in baptism. And, the Spirit comes upon us when we are converted to baptize us into our mission. The Spirit led Jesus into the wilderness to be tested by the devil. In the same manner, the Spirit sends us into those pressure points where our faith is tested.

If you want to get an idea of the kind of activity the Spirit is engaged in, look at the Spirit in Jesus' ministry and you will find a parallel in your own life.

It was through the Spirit that Jesus himself was raised from the dead.[3] Just as the presence of the Spirit was necessary for Old Testament judges, kings and prophets to do the work of the Lord, and just as it was necessary for Jesus to be empowered by the Spirit, so it is essential that the Spirit dwell in the church and in our life personally and that the Spirit does His work.

TEN WORKS OF THE SPIRIT

The Holy Spirit has a job description. In reading Scripture, you can count on finding clear descriptions of the Spirit's various tasks. Scripture does not leave the works of the Spirit to our imagination. The Spirit of God has specific work to be done and the Scripture clearly teaches us about that work.

1. The Holy Spirit exalts Jesus.

This should be listed first because it is the Spirit's first and primary work. It is the work about which He is always most concerned. Everything else the Spirit does connects with this primary task. Jesus himself said in John 15:26: "When the Counselor comes, whom I will send to you from the Father, the Spirit of truth who goes out from the Father, he will testify about me." And further, Jesus said, "He will bring glory to me by taking from what is mine and making it known to you."[4]

It is always the Spirit's mission to exalt Jesus. A long-standing criticism of Pentecostals is the false charge that we emphasize the Person and work of the Holy Spirit more than Jesus. We must be sure that is never true. The Spirit has not come so we might go away from a service talking about the gifts of the Spirit. The Spirit has come that we might be deeply impressed with the Person of Jesus Christ and go away excited about His work. The gifts are necessary to thrust us into the mission and work of Jesus. The purpose of the Spirit is to exalt Jesus and let Him be lifted up.

2. The Holy Spirit convicts us.

In John 16:8–11, Jesus identified inner conviction as the work of the Spirit:

> When he comes, he will convict the world of guilt in regard to sin and righteousness and judgment: in regard to sin, because men do not believe in me; in regard to righteousness, because I am going to the Father, where you can see me no longer; and in regard to

judgment, because the prince of this world now stands condemned.

The Holy Spirit is like the prosecuting attorney of God, but He attempts to help us before we face Judgment Day. It is the Spirit's mission to convict us in three areas. First of all, He gives us an awakened sense of sin, particularly the sin of unbelief in Jesus. The Spirit wants to reverse that unbelief so we will trust and believe in Christ.

Secondly, the Spirit wants to affirm to us the righteousness of Jesus. The Pharisees said Jesus was of the devil, but the Spirit says He is of the Father. The Holy Spirit desires to reverse the world's verdict of Jesus. The world has judged Him either as an imposter or simply one among many prophets. The Spirit's mission is to affirm the righteousness of Jesus and call on us to look to Him alone for salvation.

Lastly, the Spirit convicts of judgment that has come because the prince of this world, the evil one, has been judged by the righteousness of Jesus. The Spirit comes to usher us into an awakened sense of sin, an acknowledgement of Jesus, and an acknowledgement that judgment has already been passed against the evil one. Satan is a defeated foe.

3. The Holy Spirit regenerates us.

Jesus said, "No one can enter the kingdom of God unless he is born of water and the Spirit."[5] Spiritual regeneration comes through the Spirit's presence. Jesus acted upon this truth when, on the evening of His resurrection, He breathed upon the disciples and said to them, "Receive the Holy Spirit."[6]

Until that point, the faith of Jesus' disciples had been identical to every Old Testament saint. They looked forward to the Messiah who would one day come. But now, Jesus' work was finished on the cross and He stood before the disciples with proof that His work on the cross had merit. On that basis, they were given the opportunity no one before them had ever been given—to believe in Him who is Life, no longer with anticipatory faith but in the fact of Christ's finished work. Jesus breathed on them and gave life in a new sense. God had formed man from the dust of the ground and breathed into his nostrils the breath of life and man became a living being. Now Jesus breathed a new order of life into His disciples—eternal life.

Just as we have borne the likeness of the earthly man, so we now bear the likeness of the man of heaven.[7] Through Jesus Christ, "the law of the Spirit of life set me free from the law of sin and death."[8] I am a new person in Jesus through the Holy Spirit who has brought the life of Jesus to me.

4. The Holy Spirit lives in us.

"Don't you know that you yourselves are God's temple and that God's Spirit lives in you?"[9] These words were addressed to a church that had become insensitive to the Spirit's presence. Paul reminded that church that although they were filled with many things that are not of the Spirit, God's Spirit lived in them. The key to change involves acknowledging we are the Spirit's people.

On a personal level, Paul asked in 1 Corinthians 6:19, "Do you not know that your body is a temple of the Holy Spirit, who is in you, whom you have received from God?" He further said in 2 Thessalonians 2:13–14 that we have been sanctified through the Spirit and the fruit of His life is meant to be evident in us. We are charged to be filled with the Spirit. The alternative assumption is that we only allow the Spirit to partially dwell in us when we need to allow Him free access to every part of us.

The Spirit's presence helps us to resist the power of the evil one. In many ways, our life is somewhat like a submarine. The deeper it dives, the greater the pressure against it. Greater, therefore, must be the corresponding pressure within it to resist the evil one. We don't successfully deal with sin until we come to God and say, "Lord, fill me full of the Holy Spirit and give me the abiding presence of Jesus."

5. The Holy Spirit seals believers.

The apostle Paul wrote, "Having believed, you were marked in him with a seal, the promised Holy Spirit, who is a deposit guaranteeing our inheritance until the redemption of those who are God's possession."[10] And, "Do not grieve the Holy Spirit of God, with whom you were sealed for the day of redemption."[11]

When you become a believer, God takes His invisible stamp of ownership—the Holy Spirit—and brands your life. His presence in your life is a mark that you belong to God. Paul said the Holy Spirit is also a down payment that guarantees that you are completely Christ's.

We say a house is sold when a contract is entered into. The house is put in escrow. Then, placed on the "for sale" sign is a "sold" notice. But the house is not really sold until it has cleared escrow. Hopefully, the person who put the payment down has enough assets to complete the transaction.

To use that analogy, Paul said there is coming a day when you will be completely God's—in eternity. You are now in escrow and the Holy Spirit has sealed you and marked "saved" across your life. Of course, you can opt out through a willful decision to walk away from Christ and thereby fall away from His grace. One day, you're going to be totally out of this world and completely His. Fortunately, we don't have to worry about the good credit of the One who's buying us. His assets are sufficient. When the "sold" sign goes up over our life, it is a deposit that guarantees our redemption.

In sealing us, the Holy Spirit testifies with our spirit that we are God's children.[12] When you have sinned, it's certainly not the devil who is telling you that you are God's child. There is a still small voice that says, "Even though you have failed, there's mercy. God loves you." That's the Holy Spirit who is acting, because He has sealed you and has given you the deposit of His presence.

6. The Holy Spirit guides us.

I have never heard the voice of God audibly. But the Spirit has spoken to me. I was serving as campus pastor at Evangel College many years ago. During a tremendous revival in the fall of 1970, I was in the chapel with about one thousand students praying. I looked across the room and saw a painting of Christ on the cross that had been done by one of our students. Everything suddenly became distant, and it was just me and the painting of Christ on the cross. I felt the Spirit speak to me, "Look around here George. This isn't going to be your place of ministry much longer." It was only months later that I accepted the pastorate of a church that had just recently gone through a church split. I came to find out that they had designated the last week of October 1970 as a week of prayer and fasting before they went in search of their new pastor. They didn't know me, and I didn't know them. But the Spirit had spoken.

It was a tough start at the church, especially financially. I wondered if I'd stepped out of the will of God. Every Saturday morning, I would meet with the deacons to eat breakfast, pray and decide what bills to pay that week. One of the deacons mentioned that since I'd come, we hadn't met a single missionary financial commitment. He said, "I think we ought to take whatever comes in Sunday's offering and make at least two months missions commitments—before we pay any bills." We prayed and committed to the Lord.

Sunday came, and I never told anybody what we

were doing. At the end of the evening altar service, two deacons counted the offerings. It was $1,330 and some odd cents. I was absolutely amazed. In the prior twenty-five years, it was the second-highest offering ever received in that church. The next day I was praying and felt the Spirit speak to me, "George, I'm not interested in building this church on your personality. I'm interested in building it on Mine. Put Me front and center and I will take care of you. Put My kingdom first and I will take care of you."

Living in the Spirit is a personal relationship. When I maintain a life of prayer and communion with the Lord, I can lean on the impressions I get while I'm praying.

There are so many instances of the Spirit's guidance in Scripture. Acts 8:29 says, "The Spirit told Philip, 'Go to that chariot and stay near it.'" Also, in Acts 13:2: "The Holy Spirit said, 'Set apart for me Barnabas and Saul for the work to which I have called them.'"

We're really helpless in getting accurate guidance and direction unless the Spirit works within us. The Spirit is especially present, especially active, in junctures of our life—times when we're making vital decisions that are going to affect us for many days to come. Again and again, Scripture suggests to us that when we open ourself to God, the Spirit works in us with power and we can rest in His creative work. The Spirit knows what He is doing in assigning us our mission within His body and within His world. The Spirit doesn't make mistakes in guiding our life. We can rest in His direction.

I encourage young people, especially in moments of important decision—whether you will marry, whom you will marry, what your vocation will be, where you will go in life—how appropriate it is for you and how right it is for you to spend extended time praying that you might know what the mind of the Spirit is for your life. I can assure you, the Spirit has a purpose for you. You can choose to get ahold of that purpose and go with it, or grieve the Spirit by not spending time seeking His direction.

7. The Holy Spirit prompts us to worship.

The Spirit prompts believers to worship and adore the ever-living God. Jesus said in John 4:24 that "God is spirit, and his worshipers must worship in spirit and in truth." In Luke 10:21, Jesus himself worshipped through the Spirit, "At that time Jesus, full of joy through the Holy Spirit." Ephesians 5:18,19 admonishes us to be filled with the Spirit and to worship as we "speak to one another with psalms, hymns and spiritual songs." Paul went on to say in Ephesians 6:18, "Pray in the Spirit on all occasions with all kinds of prayers and requests."

As we take the time to worship, our spiritual well is always filled. For out of our inner man will flow rivers of living water.[13] But when we stop being responsive to the Spirit in worship, we find that almost immediately we run dry.

Pentecostal worship has always had a voluble dimension to it. We have a habit of praising the Lord together. But, sometimes it can become a mere form. As a young person, I reacted against some aspects of the Pentecostal movement, including superficial and unreal worship.

Growing up in Pentecostal churches, I reached a point in my life where I said, "Enough is enough! I'm not going to have anybody play with my emotions. I can praise God quietly. I'm a cerebral Pentecostal. I'll just think Pentecostal." But, soon I came to a different understanding.

We have verbal worship because it is scriptural. In the Bible, you find people praying aloud to God, not merely praying mentally to God. In fact, in the Book of Acts when the Spirit came on the Day of Pentecost, they were all praising God. The implication behind the text is that there was real power to their speech as they praised Him. Paul said as an act of will, "I will pray with my spirit, but I will also pray with my mind; I will sing with my spirit, but I will also sing with my mind."[14] When the Spirit comes upon us, we must choose to enter into praise when Jesus is exalted, or whether we're going to simply let that opportunity pass us by.

There's a time to be quiet in the presence of the Lord, a time to hear the Word of the Lord: "Be still, and know that I am God."[15] But there is also a time to praise the Lord with an upraised voice. There is a time to say from the depths of the inner man, "Hallelujah! For our Lord God Almighty reigns."[16]

The Spirit incites us to that kind of worship. The Spirit encourages us to be verbal. There are times in our relationship with God and as a Body when "still waters run deep." There are moments when ebullient joy is like an artesian well, and like the geyser, Old Faithful, it simply erupts with the glory and the presence of the Lord. As Spirit-filled believers, we ought to be willing to follow in whatever direction the Spirit is flowing at any given moment.

8. The Holy Spirit empowers us for witness.

Jesus said, "Do not leave Jerusalem, but wait for the gift my Father promised. . . . You will receive power when the Holy Spirit comes on you; and you will be my witnesses in Jerusalem, and in all Judea and Samaria, and to the ends of the earth."[17]

Paul said to the Thessalonians, "Our gospel came to you not simply with words, but also with power, with the Holy Spirit and with deep conviction."[18] Words are not enough. The Spirit ministers the things of Jesus to us. The Lord promised that as we go forth with the Holy Spirit to witness, the Spirit will be active in our witness and empower us for service.

There is a balance between the worship of the Lord and the work of the Lord. It is never the purpose of the Lord to simply have the Spirit stir us to worship and then leave us there. The Spirit's task is to instill strength in us in the moment of worship, so that we can go out empowered to do the work of the Lord.

I pray that the Spirit will come upon us in boldness so that whether it's in a school, an office or a neighborhood, we will dare to ask God to open doors for us. I don't know any better way to reach people for Christ than to do it the way the Holy Spirit had the Early Church do it—that is, to be filled with the Spirit and send people out to witness and do the work of the Lord.

I believe our communities can be reached with what I call the "Cornelius Connection." There was a stratum of society that the church would never have reached, an entirely separate cultural group—the upper class Gentiles. The Holy Spirit revealed the Gentiles' need for salvation to Peter's heart and, using Cornelius through whom the Spirit was working, gave a connection to bring Peter and Cornelius' household together. We need to be praying to be open to the Holy Spirit so we can connect with people and live out the Spirit's power in witness.

9. The Holy Spirit enables us to understand and apply what is taught in the Word of God.

The Spirit not only inspired the Scripture, He also caused it to be inspiring. "All scripture is God-breathed and is useful for teaching, rebuking, correcting and training in righteousness."[19] Whatever the Spirit does will line up with Scripture because the Spirit inspired Scripture to begin with. The two will always agree.

The Pentecostal movement has forgotten this at times. Many have gone off into emotional excesses, emphasizing things as *spiritual* that are not scriptural. But God has two great rivers that are flowing and they both stream out of the Spirit's presence: the river of His Word and the river of experience with Christ. And these flow together.

The Spirit causes us to understand God's Word. We see this illustrated in the story of Saint Augustine's conversion, a man who changed the shape of the church.

No one can doubt that Augustine had a genuine experience with Jesus Christ. He had dabbled in occult religions and had lived very immorally. His godly mother, Veronica, had prayed for him all his life. Then one day, as a man in his mid-thirties and burdened down with sin, he heard the voice of a child saying to him, "Take and read!" He rushed to a nook in his garden where he found a Bible lying open to Romans 13:12–14:

> The night is nearly over; the day is almost here. So let us put aside the deeds of darkness and put on the armor of light. Let us behave decently, as in the daytime, not in orgies and drunkenness, not in sexual immorality and debauchery, not in dissension and jealousy. Rather, clothe yourselves with the Lord Jesus Christ, and do not think about how to gratify the desires of the sinful nature.

Augustine read it and lived it, because the Spirit took the Word of God and made it alive.

If you're a Christian, you're a Christian because God drove His Word deep into your life. If you're growing as a Christian, it's because the Holy Spirit is faithfully applying the Word. That's His work.

10. The Holy Spirit will give life to our mortal bodies.

This is a work of the Holy Spirit that is yet to come. But the promise of that work is connected incredibly with the resurrection of Christ himself: "If the Spirit of him who raised Jesus from the dead is living in you, he who raised Christ from the dead will also give life to your mortal bodies through his Spirit, who lives in you."[20] Think of it. Paul identified that event as positive proof of the validation of the gospel and that life-giving work of the Spirit is promised to *each* of us.

RECEIVING THE SPIRIT'S FULL WORK

As a person who has always belonged to the Pentecostal movement, nothing scares me more than a group of Pentecostals going through the ritual of an ordinary Pentecostal worship service, singing the songs that have been sung for the last twenty-five years, and not being alive with what the Spirit is doing *now* in our lives. We hang a name "Pentecostal" or "Assemblies of God" on the door, as if that contributes to any reality within that church. Names don't mean anything. It's not the name we wear; it's the power we represent. It's the purity of the product. You can't label a church or institution as though it were always going to keep the Spirit. Institutions change. They grow cold, backslide and need reviving.

Each of us needs revival. Our experience with God in the past is not going to sustain us right now. We need the power of the Holy Spirit living in us every single day. It's His work today that I want—not the work of the Spirit that called me when I was a young person. Thank God for that. But I cannot last on it. I need the work of the Holy Spirit in my life today. We *all* need Him now.

Closing his article, *Five Faces of Pentecost*, Dean Merrill shares about his visit to an immigrant church in Amsterdam, Holland. It was a dynamic service, and even though he couldn't understand the language spoken, the Spirit's presence was very strong. He kept looking at a banner across the front of the sanctuary where the choir sat. It read, "Geef de Heilige Geest ruimte." He finally turned to a young man next to him and said, "Do you read Dutch?"

"Some," he replied.

"What does the sign say?" Dean asked, pointing to the stage.

He gave the translation: "Give the Holy Spirit room."

And I thought, that's right. That's what we need to do in our personal lives. That's what we need to do in our families. That's what we need to do in the body of Christ, in our church services, in our prayer meetings. It can't just be scripted. It can't just be a schedule. It can't just be, "Well, we're doing this out of routine and habit." There has to be an openness, a sense that we are making room for the Spirit. The Spirit who hovered over the chaos and breathed into it the creation, the Spirit through whom Jesus was conceived in the womb of Mary, the Spirit through whom we are born again; this creative, dynamic Spirit wants to be birthed into time and space in our lives today. In order for that to happen, we must give room for the Spirit.

1 Genesis 1:2
2 Luke 1:35
3 Romans 8:11
4 John 16:14
5 John 3:5
6 John 20:22
7 1 Corinthians 15:49
8 Romans 8:2
9 1 Corinthians 3:16
10 Ephesians 1:13,14
11 Ephesians 4:30
12 Romans 8:16
13 John 7:38, NASB
14 1 Corinthians 14:15
15 Psalm 46:10
16 Revelation 19:6
17 Acts 1:4,8
18 1 Thessalonians 1:5
19 2 Timothy 3:16
20 Romans 8:11

PASS ON A
FULL BUCKET

THESE COMMAND-

MENTS *that* I GIVE

YOU TODAY ARE *to* BE

UPON YOUR HEARTS.

IMPRESS THEM *on*

YOUR CHILDREN.

—Deuteronomy 6:6,7

PERHAPS YOU HAVE SEEN ONE OF THOSE OLD
WESTERNS where the townsfolk, threatened by a
blazing building, formed a bucket brigade from the
nearest well in order to fight the flames. A more contem-
porary example would be the lines of people at the
collapsed World Trade Center on 9/11 who passed the
rubble from person to person as they started clearing the
site. Such a tactic may seem primitive, but in some cases
it's still the only safe way to move debris from a fallen
building after a disaster.

The key to success in any bucket brigade is a full
bucket. If you slosh enough half-full buckets to the front
of the line to fight a blaze, you may just lose the building.
If you're delinquent in the amount of rubble you move
from a collapsed building, someone trapped underneath
might die.

Both the Old and New Testaments are concerned
about passing spiritual experience on to succeeding
generations. It's a task that should never be carried out
half-heartedly.

> Hear, O Israel, The Lord our God, the Lord is
> one. Love the Lord your God with all your
> heart and with all your soul and with all your
> strength. These commandments that I give
> you today are to be upon your hearts.
> Impress them on your children. Talk about
> them when you sit at home and when you
> walk along the road, when you lie down and
> when you get up. Tie them as symbols on

your hands and bind them on your fore-
heads. Write them on the doorframes of your
houses and on your gates.[1]

How can we guard the spiritual deposit that has
been entrusted to us? How can we give to our children
and grandchildren the truths and experiences with
which we were blessed? We must pass on a full bucket.

The doctrinal truths in the Assemblies of God can
never be up for grabs. Culture changes, styles of dress
change, music changes, modes of doing church change—
but our core beliefs must not change.

It's easy enough to err in either direction when
identifying the needed contents of our "full bucket."
Some seem to believe that if anything is more than four
years old, it's not relevant. Others seem to think that if
something is new, it can't be true.

Jesus described this battle between those who
would preserve the gospel and those who would destroy
it in His parable of the weeds and wheat in Matthew
13:24–30. "A man sowed good seed in his field. But while
everyone was sleeping, his enemy came and sowed weeds
among the wheat."

Notice that Jesus said, "While everyone was
sleeping." We can never let down our guard. Eternal souls
are at stake, and we do not have the luxury of self-
congratulation when the job is not completed. Every soul
reached for Christ must be discipled and matured, and
that process must continue through the generations
until He returns for His Church.

We are sleeping if . . .

• We are in a survival mode rather than a mission mode.

• We are more concerned with paying the bills than reaching the lost.

• We are depending on razzamatazz in our children's and youth programs rather than giving them sound reasons for their faith.

• We ignore the fact that up to 70 percent of our high school graduates will leave the faith within ten years of graduation.

• We move away from our originating mission of producing ministers and dedicated laypersons.

• We find our fulfillment in academic prowess and achievement rather than finding joy in the number of qualified, dedicated and trained ministers being launched into the harvest fields.

• We rely on our ingenuity, programs, methodologies of church growth, vision statements, mission statements and time runs for services—with little or no prayer and reliance on the Holy Spirit.

We must awaken and communicate the life-giving truth that every generation needs to survive. That truth is not merely a creed, not simply propositional statements or foundational truths. Our doctrine is belief in a living Lord, and that belief impacts our behavior.

If we merely maintain doctrine without mission, the water will slosh out of the bucket. Doctrine is essential, but it must be missionally communicated. And the Spirit must guide the nature of the communication. We're off mission when we lecture sinners or try to reform their behavior. Only as the Spirit speaks to hearts can our communication of doctrine come to life.

As Pentecostals, our theological reasoning and methodologies alone will not get this massive task of world evangelization done or even reach our cities or communities. We need apostolic experience as a Fellowship, as a district, as a church, as an individual. If we don't, we will spiritually die!

I believe that in our heritage we need to pass along "a full bucket" of faith and practice that Pentecostals have had for the past one hundred years. Each generation needs that same fullness of the Spirit. We began in the Spirit. We must not end up in the flesh. "Are you so foolish?" Paul asked the Galatian believers. "After beginning with the Spirit, are you now trying to attain your goal by human effort?"[2] We need to transmit to the next generation what was given to us.

Let's pass on a full bucket!

---

[1] Deuteronomy 6:4–8
[2] Galatians 3:3

T O BENEFIT FROM DR. WOOD'S INSIGHTS AND CHALLENGES, thoughtfully consider your personal life, ministry and local church:

✣ Are you seeking a continual inflow of the Spirit's power and presence in your life? In what ways do you need more of the Spirit's help?

✣ If you are a pastor or church leader, are you periodically teaching on the person and ministry of the Holy Spirit to your congregation? Are you providing opportunities for people to seek Spirit baptism?

✣ Do people from a non-Pentecostal background who visit or attend your church receive adequate teaching concerning Pentecostal faith and practice?

✣ Is praying in the Spirit a regular and consistent part of your prayer life?

✣ How is the enduring evidence of the Spirit's fullness manifested in your life?

✣ Do you depend on the Spirit's help in personal evangelism?